RECORD:
ABV calculations
Observations on fermentation
Tasting notes

From the first boil to the first taste,

The

Homebrewer's

Journal

your essential companion to brewing better beer

★ Drew Beechum ★

▲adamsmedia
Avon, Massachusetts

Published by
Adams Media, a division of F+W Media, Inc.
57 Littlefield Street, Avon, MA 02322. U.S.A.
www.adamsmedia.com

Contains material adapted and abridged from *The Everything® Homebrewing Book* by Drew Beechum, copyright © 2009 by F+W Media, Inc., ISBN 10: 1-60550-122-0, ISBN 13: 978-1-60550-122-2.

ISBN 10: 1-4405-6145-1
ISBN 13: 978-1-4405-6145-0

Printed in the United States of America.

9 8 7 6 5 4 3 2 1

This book is available at quantity discounts for bulk purchases.
For information, please call 1-800-289-0963.

Contents

The Beer

The Recipe

Preparation

Brew Day

Fermentation

Secondary Fermentation (if applicable)

Packaging

The Final Beer

Dead Simple Hefeweizen • 240

Monocle Single Hop Extra Pale Ale • 241

Plainweiser Pub Ale • 242

Chico West Coast Pale Ale • 243

Kyle's Dry Irish Stout • 244

Raucous Red West Coast Ale • 245

Frankenale • 246

JJ Remix • 248

Boat Weight Water Vapor • 250

Gatekeeper Memorial Porter • 252

Pater's Uncle Enkel • 254

Introduction

In recent years, the popularity of homebrewing has soared. It's easy to see why. First, there's the end result of your labor: bottles of beer to share with friends and family and the sounds of glasses clinking in your honor. The moment a friend looks incredulously at you and says, "You brewed this?" you'll be hooked. But there are thousands of other reasons that homebrewing has captured the imagination.

Few hobbies allow you to be as creative. It offers a chance to explore skills you never knew you had. You can learn the biology (yeast), chemistry (water and mashing), the culinary magic of flavor development, or the detective skills needed to track down obscure bits of brewing history. Brewers get the fun of their childhood chemistry set, along with the joy that any chef feels after they've tasted their creation. Brewers pay close attention to detail, and yet they have so much room to explore and improvise.

> For most of the 5,000-plus-year saga of people and beer, the beer you drank was the beer you brewed. Everyone drank beer. Everyone was a homebrewer.

Brewing also exercises your favorite skills. Your inner artist can design labels, the engineer can perfect equipment, the scientist can obsess over numbers, and the gourmet can develop exotic recipes. In other words, brewing is as scientific or creative as you want it to be. You just have to remember how you made the beer, so you can make it again!

How to Use This Journal

That's where this book comes in. Every professional brewer, big and small keeps a log for each batch. Any brewer will tell you that keeping good notes allows you to consistently make great beer. You have to make sure you're prepared—don't get caught mid-brew, realizing you missed a critical piece of the puzzle. You need to keep track of where you are—when you've added ingredients to the boil, how long you've let the beer ferment, etc.

Finally, keeping good notes on each beer is the best way to track your progress and perfect your craft. Use *The Homebrewer's Journal* to keep accurate records on your brew, from the kind of hops you choose to the last sip of your last bottle.

> **America has a long, proud tradition of homebrewing. Native Americans drank a fermented beer-like concoction made with maize. Thomas Jefferson and George Washington both had small breweries.**

Whether you're making your first batch of beer or your hundredth, this book will help you keep track of your ups and downs. That way, when a batch is award-winning, you'll be able to recreate it. And if it's not so award-winning, you can trace what might have gone wrong.

The back of *The Homebrewer's Journal* contains eleven beer recipes for inspiration. Follow them to the T, or use them as a jumping off point for your own brewing creations. Homebrewing is about reclaiming history's most popular drink, and *The Homebrewer's Journal* is the best companion a brewer can have!

Terms and Equations to Know

- **Alcohol by Weight (ABW) and Alcohol by Volume (ABV)**
  Measurement of the amount of alcohol in a drink. Since alcohol weighs less per ounce than water, ABW appears less than the equivalent ABV. For example, 3.2 percent ABW (a classic blue law in some states) is 4.0 percent ABV. Until recently, American beer was always expressed in ABW, while the rest of the world used ABV. American breweries now use ABV to sell their beer.

  To find the ABV and the ABW:
  Alcohol By Volume = (Original Gravity − Final Gravity) / 7.5
  Alcohol By Weight = (ABV) × .78

- **Alpha Acid (AA)**
  Expressed as a percentage, it's the amount of bittering acids available from hops. Dissolved in the boil, they give beer bite. Each variety of hops has an AA percentage. You can use the AA percentage of your hops variety to find the AAU of the amount you plan on adding to your recipe.

- **Alpha Acid Unit (AAU)**
  AAU is a measurement of the bitterness in the specific amount of hops you are adding to your beer, sometimes referred to as Home Brewer Unit (HBU). Here is how to find the AAU of your hops based on their weight and AA:

  AAU = Weight (hops) × AA percent (recipe)
  To scale to your current hops, divide the AAU by the new AA percent.
  Weight (needed) = AAU / AA percent (hops on hand)
  For example: Your recipe uses a half ounce of 8.1 percent AA Cascade. You can buy them at 5.4 percent AA.
  AAU = 0.5 × 8.1 = 4.05 AAU
  This, in turn, allows you to find your beer's IBU (see following).

- ## International Bittering Unit (IBU)
  When brewers talk about beer bitterness they talk about "IBUs" or international bittering units. Measurement of the amount of alpha acids dissolved. The scale runs from 0 bitterness to the human tasting threshold of 100+. This measure corresponds to bitter compound levels in the beer. The higher the number, the more bitter. Different formulas will produce different results, so all IBU calculations are a guide.

  Calculating IBUs:
  IBU (addition) = (AAU $\times$ Utilization percent $\times$ 7490) / Volume (beer)

- ## Final Gravity (FG)
  Measurement of the remaining sugars and solids in a fermented beer.

- ## Original Gravity (OG)
  Measurement of the amount of sugar dissolved in unfermented wort. Homebrewers talk about this in units of "specific gravity."

- ## Apparent Attenuation
  The difference between the FG and the OG is "apparent attenuation." Using that difference, you can calculate an approximate ABV and verify that your fermentation was healthy and complete.

  Apparent Attenuation = 100 $\times$ ((Original Gravity – Final Gravity) / Original Gravity)

- ## Wort
  The brewing term for unfermented beer.

An Example Entry

The Beer   Summer Grove Pale

Style: ___Wheat Pale Ale___

Brew Type: ☐ Extract   ☒ Extract with Steeped Grains

            ☐ Partial Mash   ☐ All Grain

The Beer Story: ___Easy-to-drink summer beer___
___with sweet wheat flavors and a___
___citrus punch.___

Desired Flavor and Aromas: ___wheat breadiness.___
___A little sweet and a big burst of grapefruit.___

Gallons: ___5.5___   SRM (Color): ___9___

OG: ___1.053___   IBUs: ___54___

ABV: ___5.5%___   Boil Time: ___60 minutes___

Ingredients

Malt/Grains/Sugar (if used)		
Amount	**Ingredient**	**Brand**
8 ounces	malt	Domestic 2-row
3/4 pound	malt	caravienne

Extract (if used)

Amount	Ingredient	Brand
8.5 pounds	Wheat Extract (liquid)	

Hops

Amount	Variety	Type	AA %	Time in Boil
0.75 ounce	Amarillo	Pellet	9.4%	60 min.
0.75 ounce	Amarillo	Pellet	9.4%	30 min.
0.75 ounce	Amarillo	Pellet	9.4%	15 min.
0.75 ounce	Amarillo	Pellet	9.4%	0 min.

Type of Water: _____ Municipal water

Water: ☐ Bottled ☐ Distilled/R.O. ☒ Filtered

Water Salts: _____ 1 teaspoon Gypsum

Other Ingredients

Amount	Ingredient	Add When?
1 tablet	Whirlfloc	15 minutes (boil)

The Recipe

Yeast: _____ WLP 001 — California Ale _____

Starter Size: **1 quart** Starter Gravity: **1.030** Days Fermented: **3**

☒ Cold Crashed

Procedures

Mash Type: ☒ Steep   ☐ Single Infusion Mash
            ☐ Step Infusion Mash   ☐ Decoction

Mash Schedule			
Step	Target Temp	Rest Time	Infusion/Direct
Steep	154	30 min.	3-quart Infusion (170°F)

Packaging

Dry Hop Schedule (if Dry Hopping)			
Amount	Variety	Temp	Days
1 ounce	Amarillo	65°F	14

Flavor Additions (e.g. vanilla, oak)	
Amount	Ingredient

Preparation

☒ Purchased all ingredients

☒ Equipment all accounted for

Total Cost: $ _____ *31.00* _____

Inventory Notes

used new brewshop for supplies —
much better selection.

Recipe Thoughts

Why choose the ingredients/techniques specified?

Wheat extract has classic wheat beer
profile (60% wheat, 40% pale).

The Caravienne is lightly sweet and
makes gorgeous orange color. Need
the pale to convert the starch.

Amarillo tastes and smells like a potent
orange and grapefruit hybrid.

Brew Day

Date: 3/1

Brewer(s): Drew

Time Started: 9 P.m.

Temperature: 91°F

☑ **Mash/Steep (if using grains)**

Grain Crush: ☐ Coarse ☐ Medium ☒ Fine ☐ Flour

Ingredient Notes (Does the malt smell fresh? Firm or mushy?): _____

fresh crush, very dry

Strike Water: Amount: 3 quarts Temperature: 170°F

Mash/Steep Temperature(s): 154°F

Type of Sparge: ☐ Fly ☒ Batch ☐ No

Sparge Water: Amount: 3 quarts Temperature: 170°F

First Runnings Gravity: N/A

Final Runnings Gravity: N/A

Notes: Topped off boil kettle to 3 gallons of wort.

Time Mash/Steep Completed: 10:15 A.M.

☑ **Boil**

Boil Vessel: 5-gallon pot

Heat Source: ☒ Gas Stove ☐ Electric Stove ☐ Propane Burner

☐ Electric Heater ☐ Other

Wort Collected: 6 quarts grain liquid and 6 quarts filtered

Initial Boil Gravity: (*Stir the boil point vigorously for a minute to ensure even sugar mixing.*) 1.039

Time to Start Boil: 10:15 A.M.

Time at Start of Boil: 10:35 A.M.

Extract Added: ☐ Start of boil ☒ Late: 15 minutes

☒ Scum Skimmed

Boil Notes (vigor, etc): Roiling — need turkey fryer for anything larger

Hops (as needed)

☒ __60__ Minute Addition   ☐ _____ Minute Addition

☒ __30__ Minute Addition   ☐ _____ Minute Addition

☒ __15__ Minute Addition   ☐ _____ Minute Addition

☒ __0__ Minute Addition

Notes: __1st addition kicked up foam, added a little__
__cold water.__

☐ Adding Other Ingredients

Notes: __N/A__

Time Boil Ended: __11:35 A.M.__

☒ Whirlpool

How Long?: __10 minutes__

☒ Chill Wort

Cooling Mechanism: ☐ Closed Pot Overnight   ☒ Sink/Ice Bath

☐ Immersion Coil   ☐ Whirlpool Immersion   ☐ Counterflow Chiller

Chilling Start Time: __11:45 A.M.__

Water/Bath Temperature: __50°F__

Temperature of Wort when Fully Chilled: __65°F__

Chilling Finish Time: __1 P.M.__

☒ Hydrometer Reading:

Original gravity (O.G.) __1.054__

☒ Notes on pitching the yeast

__Decanted most of the starter wort.__

Temperature of the wort when the yeast is pitched: __65°F__

☒ Used Starter

☒ Decanted Starter

Brew Day Finished: __1:15 P.M.__

Fermentation

Date: _____ 3/1 _____

Fermenter Type: ☒ Bucket ☐ Glass Carboy ☐ Plastic Carboy
☐ Keg ☐ Conical ☐ Other: _____

Fermenter Closure: ☒ Airlock ☐ Blow-off Tube ☐ Foil Cap ☐ Open

Length of Ferment: _____ 5 _____ Days

Aroma and Visual Notes: _____ Rocky head, so airlock
didn't bubble at first. Lid wasn't
sealed perfectly. Tightened lid
Solved airlock issue.

Ferment Temperature

Try to keep the temperature constant throughout the ferment.

Date: _____ 3/1 _____ Temp: _____ 67°F _____
Date: _____ 3/3 _____ Temp: _____ 68°F _____
Date: _____ 3/5 _____ Temp: _____ 65°F _____
Date: _____ Temp: _____

Secondary Fermentation (if applicable)

Date: _____ 3/6 _____

Gravity at Transfer: _____ 1.015 _____

Length of Ferment: _____ 14 _____ Days

Aroma and Visual Notes: _____ Sweet, bready, spicy,
mixed with grapefruit scent.

Additions to Secondary: _____ Dry hops _____

Finings/Clarification Aids: _____ N/A _____

Packaging

Date: _____ **3/20** _____

Hydrometer Reading: _____ **1.012** _____
(This number is the Final Gravity, or FG).

Calculate Alcohol by Volume (or ABV):

$$\underset{\text{Alcohol By Volume}}{\underline{\textbf{5.73}}} = (\underset{\text{Original Gravity}}{\underline{\textbf{55}}} - \underset{\text{Final Gravity}}{\underline{\textbf{12}}}) / 7.5$$

Calculating Attenuation

$$\underset{\text{Apparent Attenuation}}{\underline{\textbf{78\%}}} = 100 \times ((\underset{\text{Original Gravity}}{\underline{\textbf{55}}} - \underset{\text{Final Gravity}}{\underline{\textbf{12}}}) / \underset{\text{Original Gravity}}{\underline{\textbf{55}}})$$

PACKAGE

☒ Bottle   ☐ Keg

CARBONATION

Desired Level of Carbonation: _____ **2.5 volumes** _____

☒ Primed

with (sugar, wort, etc): _____ **corn sugar** _____

How much: _____ **3 ounces (by weight)** _____

☐ Forced

Beer Temp: _____

CO_2 Setting: _____ p.s.i.

Method: ☐ Steady Pressure _____ week(s)

☐ Fast Carbonation: Shake at _____ p.s.i. for _____ minutes

Beer Storage Temperature: _____ **65°F** _____

The Final Beer

Chill and test a bottle. If carbonated, you're ready! Otherwise, wait another week and repeat. As you take notes, record how the beer changes as it warms up and lets off more CO_2.

Beer Temperature: _____ _48°F_ _____

Pour Notes (carbonation, head, cloudy, etc.): _Big poof of_
rocky head.

Aroma Notes (What do you smell from the hops, the malt and the yeast?) _____
Like sweetrolls with marmalade.

Appearance Notes (clarity, color, etc.)
Bright orangy body.

Taste Notes (What tastes do you perceive from the ingredients?)
Sweet wheat — oranges from the hops,
toastiness from the Caravienne?

Mouth Feel/Finish
Round and lush, but not sugary.
Hops pack enough bitterness to clear the tongue.

Overall Notes
Good beer! must make more!

Circle all that apply

Bitter   Buttery   Cooked   Sweet   (Hoppy)   (Fruity)   Harsh   Malty   Metallic
Spicy   Roasted   Smoky   Watery   Yeasty   Acidic   Sour   (Clean)   Earthy

Impressions that Change with Temperature/Time: _Aroma changed_
with floral notes appearing.

What Worked? _Everything!_

What Didn't Work? __N/A__

What Changes Do I Want to Make? __Make a bigger, more__
__aggressive version.__

Overall Score (0–50) __40__

Competition Notes (If you enter the beer in a competition, record the judges' impressions and scores.)

Competition Name: __Mayfaire__
Date: __April__   Score: __39__   Award: __1st__
Judge Notes: __Clean. Bitterness provides the__
__right level of punch. Could use__
__better clarity.__

Competition Name: __NHC__
Date: __May__   Score: __41__   Award: __2nd__
Judge Notes: __Clear, sweet, but not overall.__
__Grass, herbal notes from the dry hop.__
__Some minor staleness is creeping in.__

Competition Name: __LA County Faire__
Date: __August__   Score: __30__   Award: __N/A__
Judge Notes: __Beer is fading. Hops are less__
__prominent. There is a brown-sugar__
__flavor. The beer is too old for__
__its strength.__
Competition Name: _____
Date: _____ Score: _____ Award: _____
Judge Notes: _____

The Beer Oh honey my Nut, Brown.

Style: Brown Ale

Brew Type: ☐ Extract   ☑ Extract with Steeped Grains
           ☐ Partial Mash ☐ All Grain

The Beer Story: _____
   Jeff in town. We like beer.
   We made Beer. We drank beer.
_____

Desired Flavor and Aromas: honey, nuts, & Love
_____

Gallons: 5   SRM (Color): Brown
OG: _____   IBUs: _____
ABV: _____   Boil Time: 60

Ingredients

Malt/Grains/Sugar (if used)		
Amount	Ingredient	Brand
3 #	Amber DME	Briess
3 #	Dark DME	
2 oz	Vanguard	

Extract (if used)

Amount	Ingredient	Brand

Hops

Amount	Variety	Type	AA %	Time in Boil
1.5	Vanguard		4.9	60
.5	Vanguard			flame out

Type of Water: __SD Tap !__

Water: ☐ Bottled   ☐ Distilled/R.O.   ☐ Filtered

Water Salts: _____

Other Ingredients

Amount	Ingredient	Add When?
1 tab	Merry Whilfloc	10 min

The Recipe

Yeast: _White Labr – Dry English_

Starter Size: _5g_____ Starter Gravity: _____ Days Fermented: _____

☐ Cold Crashed

Procedures

Mash Type: ☑ Steep   ☐ Single Infusion Mash
                ☐ Step Infusion Mash   ☐ Decoction

Mash Schedule			
Step	Target Temp	Rest Time	Infusion/Direct

Packaging

Dry Hop Schedule (if Dry Hopping)			
Amount	Variety	Temp	Days

Flavor Additions (e.g. vanilla, oak)	
Amount	Ingredient

Preparation

☐ Purchased all ingredients

☐ Equipment all accounted for

Total Cost: $ _____41_____

Inventory Notes

_____
_____
_____
_____
_____
_____
_____
_____

Recipe Thoughts

Why choose the ingredients/techniques specified?

_____
_____
_____
_____
_____
_____
_____
_____
_____
_____
_____
_____
_____
_____

Brew Day

Date: __5/29/14__

Brewer(s): __Dustin · Jeff__

Time Started: __1:30 pm__

Temperature: __64__

☑ Mash/Steep (if using grains)

Grain Crush: ☑ Coarse   ☑ Medium   ☐ Fine   ☐ Flour

Ingredient Notes (Does the malt smell fresh? Firm or mushy?): _____
_____ So Fresh _____

Strike Water: Amount: _____   Temperature: _____

Mash/Steep Temperature(s): _____

Type of Sparge: ☐ Fly   ☐ Batch   ☐ No

Sparge Water: Amount: _____   Temperature: _____

First Runnings Gravity: _____

Final Runnings Gravity: _____

Notes: _____
_____
_____

Time Mash/Steep Completed: _____

☑ Boil

Boil Vessel: __Pot__

Heat Source: ☐ Gas Stove   ☑ Electric Stove   ☐ Propane Burner
              ☐ Electric Heater   ☐ Other

Wort Collected: _____

Initial Boil Gravity: (*Stir the boil point vigorously for a minute to ensure even sugar mixing.*) _____

Time to Start Boil: _____

Time at Start of Boil: _____

Extract Added: ☐ Start of boil   ☐ Late: _____ minutes

☐ Scum Skimmed

Boil Notes (vigor, etc): _____
_____

Hops (as needed)

☐ _____ Minute Addition   ☐ _____ Minute Addition

☐ _____ Minute Addition   ☐ _____ Minute Addition

☐ _____ Minute Addition   ☐ _____ Minute Addition

☐ _____ Minute Addition

Notes: _____

_____

_____

☐ Adding Other Ingredients

Notes: _____

_____

_____

Time Boil Ended: _____

☐ Whirlpool

How Long?: _____

☐ Chill Wort

Cooling Mechanism: ☐ Closed Pot Overnight   ☐ Sink/Ice Bath

☐ Immersion Coil   ☐ Whirlpool Immersion   ☐ Counterflow Chiller

Chilling Start Time: _____

Water/Bath Temperature: _____

Temperature of Wort when Fully Chilled: _____

Chilling Finish Time: _____

☐ Hydrometer Reading:

    Original gravity (O.G.) _____

☐ Notes on pitching the yeast

_____

_____

_____

Temperature of the wort when the yeast is pitched: _____

☐ Used Starter

☐ Decanted Starter

Brew Day Finished: _____

Fermentation

Date: _____

Fermenter Type: ☐ Bucket   ☐ Glass Carboy   ☐ Plastic Carboy

☐ Keg   ☐ Conical   ☐ Other: _____

Fermenter Closure: ☐ Airlock   ☐ Blow-off Tube   ☐ Foil Cap   ☐ Open

Length of Ferment: _____ Days

Aroma and Visual Notes: _____

_____

_____

_____

Ferment Temperature

Try to keep the temperature constant throughout the ferment.

Date: _____ Temp: _____

Date: _____ Temp: _____

Date: _____ Temp: _____

Date: _____ Temp: _____

Secondary Fermentation (if applicable)

Date: _____

Gravity at Transfer: _____

Length of Ferment: _____ Days

Aroma and Visual Notes: _____

_____

_____

_____

Additions to Secondary: _____

_____

_____

Finings/Clarification Aids: _____

_____

_____

Packaging

Date: _____

Hydrometer Reading: _____
(This number is the Final Gravity, or FG).

Calculate Alcohol by Volume (or ABV):

$$\underset{\text{Alcohol By Volume}}{\underline{\hspace{3cm}}} = (\underset{\text{Original Gravity}}{\underline{\hspace{3cm}}} - \underset{\text{Final Gravity}}{\underline{\hspace{3cm}}}) / 7.5$$

Calculating Attenuation

$$\underset{\text{Apparent Attenuation}}{\underline{\hspace{3cm}}} = 100 \times ((\underset{\text{Original Gravity}}{\underline{\hspace{3cm}}} - \underset{\text{Final Gravity}}{\underline{\hspace{3cm}}}) / \underset{\text{Original Gravity}}{\underline{\hspace{3cm}}})$$

PACKAGE

☐ Bottle   ☐ Keg

CARBONATION

Desired Level of Carbonation: _____

☐ Primed

   with (sugar, wort, etc): _____

How much: _____

☐ Forced

Beer Temp: _____

CO_2 Setting: _____ p.s.i.

Method: ☐ Steady Pressure _____ week(s)

   ☐ Fast Carbonation: Shake at _____ p.s.i. for _____ minutes

Beer Storage Temperature: _____

The Final Beer

Chill and test a bottle. If carbonated, you're ready! Otherwise, wait another week and repeat. As you take notes, record how the beer changes as it warms up and lets off more CO_2.

Beer Temperature: _____

Pour Notes (carbonation, head, cloudy, etc.): _____

Aroma Notes (What do you smell from the hops, the malt and the yeast?) _____

Appearance Notes (clarity, color, etc.)

Taste Notes (What tastes do you perceive from the ingredients?)

Mouth Feel/Finish

Overall Notes

Circle all that apply

Bitter   Buttery   Cooked   Sweet   Hoppy   Fruity   Harsh   Malty   Metallic

Spicy   Roasted   Smoky   Watery   Yeasty   Acidic   Sour   Clean   Earthy

Impressions that Change with Temperature/Time: _____

What Worked? _____

What Didn't Work? _____

_____

What Changes Do I Want to Make? _____

_____

_____

Overall Score (0–50) _____

Competition Notes (If you enter the beer in a competition, record the judges' impressions and scores.)

Competition Name: _____

Date: _____ Score: _____ Award: _____

Judge Notes: _____

_____

_____

_____

Competition Name: _____

Date: _____ Score: _____ Award: _____

Judge Notes: _____

_____

_____

_____

Competition Name: _____

Date: _____ Score: _____ Award: _____

Judge Notes: _____

_____

_____

_____

Competition Name: _____

Date: _____ Score: _____ Award: _____

Judge Notes: _____

_____

_____

_____

The Beer

Style: _____

Brew Type: ☐ Extract   ☐ Extract with Steeped Grains
            ☐ Partial Mash   ☐ All Grain

The Beer Story: _____

_____

_____

_____

_____

Desired Flavor and Aromas: _____

_____

_____

Gallons: _____ SRM (Color): _____

OG: _____ IBUs: _____

ABV: _____ Boil Time: _____

Ingredients

Malt/Grains/Sugar (if used)		
Amount	Ingredient	Brand

Extract (if used)		
Amount	Ingredient	Brand

Hops				
Amount	Variety	Type	AA %	Time in Boil

Type of Water: _____

Water: ☐ Bottled   ☐ Distilled/R.O.   ☐ Filtered

Water Salts: _____

Other Ingredients		
Amount	Ingredient	Add When?

The Recipe

Yeast: _____

_____

Starter Size: _____ Starter Gravity: _____ Days Fermented: _____

☐ Cold Crashed

Procedures

Mash Type: ☐ Steep   ☐ Single Infusion Mash
          ☐ Step Infusion Mash   ☐ Decoction

Mash Schedule			
Step	Target Temp	Rest Time	Infusion/Direct

Packaging

Dry Hop Schedule (if Dry Hopping)			
Amount	Variety	Temp	Days

Flavor Additions (e.g. vanilla, oak)	
Amount	Ingredient

Preparation

☐ Purchased all ingredients

☐ Equipment all accounted for

Total Cost: $ _____

Inventory Notes

_____

_____

_____

_____

_____

_____

_____

Recipe Thoughts

Why choose the ingredients/techniques specified?

_____

_____

_____

_____

_____

_____

_____

_____

_____

_____

_____

_____

_____

_____

Brew Day

Date: _____

Brewer(s): _____

Time Started: _____

Temperature: _____

☐ Mash/Steep (if using grains)

Grain Crush:　☐ Coarse　☐ Medium　☐ Fine　☐ Flour

Ingredient Notes (Does the malt smell fresh? Firm or mushy?): _____

_____

Strike Water: Amount: _____　Temperature: _____

Mash/Steep Temperature(s): _____

Type of Sparge:　☐ Fly　☐ Batch　☐ No

Sparge Water: Amount: _____　Temperature: _____

First Runnings Gravity: _____

Final Runnings Gravity: _____

Notes: _____

_____

_____

Time Mash/Steep Completed: _____

☐ Boil

Boil Vessel: _____

Heat Source:　☐ Gas Stove　　　☐ Electric Stove　　　☐ Propane Burner

　　　　　　　　☐ Electric Heater　☐ Other

Wort Collected: _____

Initial Boil Gravity: (*Stir the boil point vigorously for a minute to ensure even sugar mixing.*) _____

Time to Start Boil: _____

Time at Start of Boil: _____

Extract Added: ☐ Start of boil　☐ Late: _____ minutes

☐ Scum Skimmed

Boil Notes (vigor, etc): _____

_____

Hops (as needed)

☐ _____ Minute Addition   ☐ _____ Minute Addition
☐ _____ Minute Addition   ☐ _____ Minute Addition
☐ _____ Minute Addition   ☐ _____ Minute Addition
☐ _____ Minute Addition

Notes: _____

_____

_____

☐ Adding Other Ingredients

Notes: _____

_____

_____

Time Boil Ended: _____

☐ Whirlpool

How Long?: _____

☐ Chill Wort

Cooling Mechanism: ☐ Closed Pot Overnight   ☐ Sink/Ice Bath
☐ Immersion Coil   ☐ Whirlpool Immersion   ☐ Counterflow Chiller

Chilling Start Time: _____

Water/Bath Temperature: _____

Temperature of Wort when Fully Chilled: _____

Chilling Finish Time: _____

☐ Hydrometer Reading:

    Original gravity (O.G.) _____

☐ Notes on pitching the yeast

_____

_____

_____

Temperature of the wort when the yeast is pitched: _____

☐ Used Starter

☐ Decanted Starter

Brew Day Finished: _____

Fermentation

Date: _____

Fermenter Type: ☐ Bucket ☐ Glass Carboy ☐ Plastic Carboy

  ☐ Keg ☐ Conical ☐ Other: _____

Fermenter Closure: ☐ Airlock ☐ Blow-off Tube ☐ Foil Cap ☐ Open

Length of Ferment: _____ Days

Aroma and Visual Notes: _____

_____

_____

_____

Ferment Temperature

Try to keep the temperature constant throughout the ferment.

Date: _____ Temp: _____

Date: _____ Temp: _____

Date: _____ Temp: _____

Date: _____ Temp: _____

Secondary Fermentation (if applicable)

Date: _____

Gravity at Transfer: _____

Length of Ferment: _____ Days

Aroma and Visual Notes: _____

_____

_____

_____

Additions to Secondary: _____

_____

_____

Finings/Clarification Aids: _____

_____

_____

Packaging

Date: _____

Hydrometer Reading: _____
(This number is the Final Gravity, or FG).

Calculate Alcohol by Volume (or ABV):

$$\underset{\text{Alcohol By Volume}}{\underline{\hspace{3cm}}} = (\underset{\text{Original Gravity}}{\underline{\hspace{3cm}}} - \underset{\text{Final Gravity}}{\underline{\hspace{3cm}}}) / 7.5$$

Calculating Attenuation

$$\underset{\text{Apparent Attenuation}}{\underline{\hspace{3cm}}} = 100 \times ((\underset{\text{Original Gravity}}{\underline{\hspace{3cm}}} - \underset{\text{Final Gravity}}{\underline{\hspace{3cm}}}) / \underset{\text{Original Gravity}}{\underline{\hspace{3cm}}})$$

PACKAGE

☐ Bottle   ☐ Keg

CARBONATION

Desired Level of Carbonation: _____

☐ Primed

    with (sugar, wort, etc): _____

How much: _____

☐ Forced

Beer Temp: _____

CO_2 Setting: _____ p.s.i.

Method: ☐ Steady Pressure _____ week(s)

    ☐ Fast Carbonation: Shake at _____ p.s.i. for _____ minutes

Beer Storage Temperature: _____

The Final Beer

Chill and test a bottle. If carbonated, you're ready! Otherwise, wait another week and repeat. As you take notes, record how the beer changes as it warms up and lets off more CO_2.

Beer Temperature: _____

Pour Notes (carbonation, head, cloudy, etc.): _____

_____

Aroma Notes (What do you smell from the hops, the malt and the yeast?) _____

_____

_____

Appearance Notes (clarity, color, etc.)

_____

_____

Taste Notes (What tastes do you perceive from the ingredients?)

_____

_____

Mouth Feel/Finish

_____

_____

Overall Notes

_____

_____

Circle all that apply

Bitter   Buttery   Cooked   Sweet   Hoppy   Fruity   Harsh   Malty   Metallic

Spicy   Roasted   Smoky   Watery   Yeasty   Acidic   Sour   Clean   Earthy

Impressions that Change with Temperature/Time: _____

_____

What Worked? _____

_____

What Didn't Work? _____

_____

What Changes Do I Want to Make? _____

_____

_____

Overall Score (0–50) _____

Competition Notes (If you enter the beer in a competition, record the judges' impressions and scores.)

Competition Name: _____

Date: _____ Score: _____ Award: _____

Judge Notes: _____

_____

_____

_____

Competition Name: _____

Date: _____ Score: _____ Award: _____

Judge Notes: _____

_____

_____

_____

Competition Name: _____

Date: _____ Score: _____ Award: _____

Judge Notes: _____

_____

_____

_____

Competition Name: _____

Date: _____ Score: _____ Award: _____

Judge Notes: _____

_____

_____

_____

The Beer

Style: _____

Brew Type: ☐ Extract ☐ Extract with Steeped Grains
☐ Partial Mash ☐ All Grain

The Beer Story: _____

_____

_____

_____

_____

Desired Flavor and Aromas: _____

_____

_____

Gallons: _____ SRM (Color): _____

OG: _____ IBUs: _____

ABV: _____ Boil Time: _____

Ingredients

Malt/Grains/Sugar (if used)		
Amount	Ingredient	Brand

Extract (if used)		
Amount	Ingredient	Brand

Hops				
Amount	Variety	Type	AA %	Time in Boil

Type of Water: _____

Water: ☐ Bottled   ☐ Distilled/R.O.   ☐ Filtered

Water Salts: _____

Other Ingredients		
Amount	Ingredient	Add When?

The Recipe

Yeast: _____

_____

Starter Size: _____ Starter Gravity: _____ Days Fermented: _____

☐ Cold Crashed

Procedures

Mash Type: ☐ Steep   ☐ Single Infusion Mash
           ☐ Step Infusion Mash   ☐ Decoction

Mash Schedule			
Step	Target Temp	Rest Time	Infusion/Direct

Packaging

Dry Hop Schedule (if Dry Hopping)			
Amount	Variety	Temp	Days

Flavor Additions (e.g. vanilla, oak)	
Amount	Ingredient

Preparation

☐ Purchased all ingredients

☐ Equipment all accounted for

Total Cost: $ _____

Inventory Notes

_____
_____
_____
_____
_____
_____
_____
_____

Recipe Thoughts

Why choose the ingredients/techniques specified?

_____
_____
_____
_____
_____
_____
_____
_____
_____
_____
_____
_____
_____
_____

Brew Day

Date: _____

Brewer(s): _____

Time Started: _____

Temperature: _____

☐ Mash/Steep (if using grains)

Grain Crush: ☐ Coarse ☐ Medium ☐ Fine ☐ Flour

Ingredient Notes (Does the malt smell fresh? Firm or mushy?): _____

_____

Strike Water: Amount: _____ Temperature: _____

Mash/Steep Temperature(s): _____

Type of Sparge: ☐ Fly ☐ Batch ☐ No

Sparge Water: Amount: _____ Temperature: _____

First Runnings Gravity: _____

Final Runnings Gravity: _____

Notes: _____

_____

_____

Time Mash/Steep Completed: _____

☐ Boil

Boil Vessel: _____

Heat Source: ☐ Gas Stove   ☐ Electric Stove   ☐ Propane Burner

☐ Electric Heater   ☐ Other

Wort Collected: _____

Initial Boil Gravity: (*Stir the boil point vigorously for a minute to ensure even sugar mixing.*) _____

Time to Start Boil: _____

Time at Start of Boil: _____

Extract Added: ☐ Start of boil ☐ Late: _____ minutes

☐ Scum Skimmed

Boil Notes (vigor, etc): _____

_____

Hops (as needed)

☐ _____ Minute Addition   ☐ _____ Minute Addition

☐ _____ Minute Addition   ☐ _____ Minute Addition

☐ _____ Minute Addition   ☐ _____ Minute Addition

☐ _____ Minute Addition

Notes: _____

_____

_____

☐ Adding Other Ingredients

Notes: _____

_____

_____

Time Boil Ended: _____

☐ Whirlpool

How Long?: _____

☐ Chill Wort

Cooling Mechanism: ☐ Closed Pot Overnight   ☐ Sink/Ice Bath

☐ Immersion Coil   ☐ Whirlpool Immersion   ☐ Counterflow Chiller

Chilling Start Time: _____

Water/Bath Temperature: _____

Temperature of Wort when Fully Chilled: _____

Chilling Finish Time: _____

☐ Hydrometer Reading:

    Original gravity (O.G.) _____

☐ Notes on pitching the yeast

_____

_____

_____

Temperature of the wort when the yeast is pitched: _____

☐ Used Starter

☐ Decanted Starter

Brew Day Finished: _____

Fermentation

Date: _____

Fermenter Type: ☐ Bucket ☐ Glass Carboy ☐ Plastic Carboy
☐ Keg ☐ Conical ☐ Other: _____

Fermenter Closure: ☐ Airlock ☐ Blow-off Tube ☐ Foil Cap ☐ Open

Length of Ferment: _____ Days

Aroma and Visual Notes: _____
_____
_____
_____

Ferment Temperature

Try to keep the temperature constant throughout the ferment.

Date: _____ Temp: _____
Date: _____ Temp: _____
Date: _____ Temp: _____
Date: _____ Temp: _____

Secondary Fermentation (if applicable)

Date: _____

Gravity at Transfer: _____

Length of Ferment: _____ Days

Aroma and Visual Notes: _____
_____
_____
_____

Additions to Secondary: _____
_____
_____

Finings/Clarification Aids: _____
_____
_____

Packaging

Date: _____

Hydrometer Reading: _____
(This number is the Final Gravity, or FG).

Calculate Alcohol by Volume (or ABV):

$$\underset{\text{Alcohol By Volume}}{\underline{\hspace{3cm}}} = (\underset{\text{Original Gravity}}{\underline{\hspace{3cm}}} - \underset{\text{Final Gravity}}{\underline{\hspace{3cm}}}) / 7.5$$

Calculating Attenuation

$$\underset{\text{Apparent Attenuation}}{\underline{\hspace{3cm}}} = 100 \times ((\underset{\text{Original Gravity}}{\underline{\hspace{3cm}}} - \underset{\text{Final Gravity}}{\underline{\hspace{3cm}}}) / \underset{\text{Original Gravity}}{\underline{\hspace{3cm}}})$$

PACKAGE

☐ Bottle   ☐ Keg

CARBONATION

Desired Level of Carbonation: _____

☐ Primed

   with (sugar, wort, etc): _____

How much: _____

☐ Forced

Beer Temp: _____

CO_2 Setting: _____ p.s.i.

Method: ☐ Steady Pressure _____ week(s)

          ☐ Fast Carbonation: Shake at _____ p.s.i. for _____ minutes

Beer Storage Temperature: _____

The Final Beer

Chill and test a bottle. If carbonated, you're ready! Otherwise, wait another week and repeat. As you take notes, record how the beer changes as it warms up and lets off more CO_2.

Beer Temperature: _____

Pour Notes (carbonation, head, cloudy, etc.): _____

_____

Aroma Notes (What do you smell from the hops, the malt and the yeast?) _____

_____

_____

Appearance Notes (clarity, color, etc.)

_____

_____

Taste Notes (What tastes do you perceive from the ingredients?)

_____

_____

Mouth Feel/Finish

_____

_____

Overall Notes

_____

_____

_____

Circle all that apply

Bitter   Buttery   Cooked   Sweet   Hoppy   Fruity   Harsh   Malty   Metallic
Spicy   Roasted   Smoky   Watery   Yeasty   Acidic   Sour   Clean   Earthy

Impressions that Change with Temperature/Time: _____

_____

What Worked? _____

_____

What Didn't Work? _____

_____

What Changes Do I Want to Make? _____

_____

_____

Overall Score (0–50) _____

Competition Notes (If you enter the beer in a competition, record the judges' impressions and scores.)

Competition Name: _____
Date: _____ Score: _____ Award: _____
Judge Notes: _____

_____

_____

_____

Competition Name: _____
Date: _____ Score: _____ Award: _____
Judge Notes: _____

_____

_____

_____

Competition Name: _____
Date: _____ Score: _____ Award: _____
Judge Notes: _____

_____

_____

_____

Competition Name: _____
Date: _____ Score: _____ Award: _____
Judge Notes: _____

_____

_____

_____

The Beer

Style: _____

Brew Type: ☐ Extract   ☐ Extract with Steeped Grains
            ☐ Partial Mash   ☐ All Grain

The Beer Story: _____

_____

_____

_____

_____

Desired Flavor and Aromas: _____

_____

_____

Gallons: _____   SRM (Color): _____
OG: _____   IBUs: _____
ABV: _____   Boil Time: _____

Ingredients

Malt/Grains/Sugar (if used)		
Amount	Ingredient	Brand

Extract (if used)		
Amount	Ingredient	Brand

Hops				
Amount	Variety	Type	AA %	Time in Boil

Type of Water: _____

Water: ☐ Bottled   ☐ Distilled/R.O.   ☐ Filtered

Water Salts: _____

Other Ingredients		
Amount	Ingredient	Add When?

The Recipe

Yeast: _____

_____

Starter Size: _____ Starter Gravity: _____ Days Fermented: _____

☐ Cold Crashed

Procedures

Mash Type: ☐ Steep   ☐ Single Infusion Mash
            ☐ Step Infusion Mash   ☐ Decoction

Mash Schedule			
Step	Target Temp	Rest Time	Infusion/Direct

Packaging

Dry Hop Schedule (if Dry Hopping)			
Amount	Variety	Temp	Days

Flavor Additions (e.g. vanilla, oak)	
Amount	Ingredient

Preparation

☐ Purchased all ingredients

☐ Equipment all accounted for

Total Cost: $ _____

Inventory Notes

_____

_____

_____

_____

_____

_____

_____

Recipe Thoughts

Why choose the ingredients/techniques specified?

_____

_____

_____

_____

_____

_____

_____

_____

_____

_____

_____

_____

_____

_____

Brew Day

Date: _____

Brewer(s): _____

Time Started: _____

Temperature: _____

☐ **Mash/Steep (if using grains)**

Grain Crush: ☐ Coarse ☐ Medium ☐ Fine ☐ Flour

Ingredient Notes (Does the malt smell fresh? Firm or mushy?): _____

_____

Strike Water: Amount: _____ Temperature: _____

Mash/Steep Temperature(s): _____

Type of Sparge: ☐ Fly ☐ Batch ☐ No

Sparge Water: Amount: _____ Temperature: _____

First Runnings Gravity: _____

Final Runnings Gravity: _____

Notes: _____

_____

_____

Time Mash/Steep Completed: _____

☐ **Boil**

Boil Vessel: _____

Heat Source: ☐ Gas Stove ☐ Electric Stove ☐ Propane Burner

　　　　　　　 ☐ Electric Heater ☐ Other

Wort Collected: _____

Initial Boil Gravity: (*Stir the boil point vigorously for a minute to ensure even sugar mixing.*) _____

Time to Start Boil: _____

Time at Start of Boil: _____

Extract Added: ☐ Start of boil ☐ Late: _____ minutes

☐ Scum Skimmed

Boil Notes (vigor, etc): _____

_____

Hops (as needed)

☐ _____ Minute Addition ☐ _____ Minute Addition

☐ _____ Minute Addition ☐ _____ Minute Addition

☐ _____ Minute Addition ☐ _____ Minute Addition

☐ _____ Minute Addition

Notes: _____

_____

_____

☐ Adding Other Ingredients

Notes: _____

_____

_____

Time Boil Ended: _____

☐ Whirlpool

How Long?: _____

☐ Chill Wort

Cooling Mechanism: ☐ Closed Pot Overnight ☐ Sink/Ice Bath

☐ Immersion Coil ☐ Whirlpool Immersion ☐ Counterflow Chiller

Chilling Start Time: _____

Water/Bath Temperature: _____

Temperature of Wort when Fully Chilled: _____

Chilling Finish Time: _____

☐ Hydrometer Reading:

Original gravity (O.G.) _____

☐ Notes on pitching the yeast

_____

_____

_____

Temperature of the wort when the yeast is pitched: _____

☐ Used Starter

☐ Decanted Starter

Brew Day Finished: _____

Fermentation

Date: _____

Fermenter Type: ☐ Bucket   ☐ Glass Carboy   ☐ Plastic Carboy

                ☐ Keg   ☐ Conical   ☐ Other: _____

Fermenter Closure: ☐ Airlock   ☐ Blow-off Tube   ☐ Foil Cap   ☐ Open

Length of Ferment: _____ Days

Aroma and Visual Notes: _____

_____

_____

_____

Ferment Temperature

Try to keep the temperature constant throughout the ferment.

Date: _____ Temp: _____

Date: _____ Temp: _____

Date: _____ Temp: _____

Date: _____ Temp: _____

Secondary Fermentation (if applicable)

Date: _____

Gravity at Transfer: _____

Length of Ferment: _____ Days

Aroma and Visual Notes: _____

_____

_____

_____

Additions to Secondary: _____

_____

_____

Finings/Clarification Aids: _____

_____

_____

Packaging

Date: _____

Hydrometer Reading: _____
(This number is the Final Gravity, or FG).

Calculate Alcohol by Volume (or ABV):

$$\underset{\text{Alcohol By Volume}}{\underline{\hspace{3cm}}} = (\underset{\text{Original Gravity}}{\underline{\hspace{3cm}}} - \underset{\text{Final Gravity}}{\underline{\hspace{3cm}}}) / 7.5$$

Calculating Attenuation

$$\underset{\text{Apparent Attenuation}}{\underline{\hspace{3cm}}} = 100 \times ((\underset{\text{Original Gravity}}{\underline{\hspace{2.5cm}}} - \underset{\text{Final Gravity}}{\underline{\hspace{2.5cm}}}) / \underset{\text{Original Gravity}}{\underline{\hspace{2.5cm}}})$$

PACKAGE

☐ Bottle   ☐ Keg

CARBONATION

Desired Level of Carbonation: _____

☐ Primed

    with (sugar, wort, etc): _____

How much: _____

☐ Forced

Beer Temp: _____

CO_2 Setting: _____ p.s.i.

Method: ☐ Steady Pressure _____ week(s)

        ☐ Fast Carbonation: Shake at _____ p.s.i. for _____ minutes

Beer Storage Temperature: _____

The Final Beer

Chill and test a bottle. If carbonated, you're ready! Otherwise, wait another week and repeat. As you take notes, record how the beer changes as it warms up and lets off more CO_2.

Beer Temperature: _____

Pour Notes (carbonation, head, cloudy, etc.): _____

_____

Aroma Notes (What do you smell from the hops, the malt and the yeast?) _____

_____

_____

Appearance Notes (clarity, color, etc.)

_____

_____

Taste Notes (What tastes do you perceive from the ingredients?)

_____

_____

Mouth Feel/Finish

_____

_____

Overall Notes

_____

_____

_____

Circle all that apply

Bitter   Buttery   Cooked   Sweet   Hoppy   Fruity   Harsh   Malty   Metallic

Spicy   Roasted   Smoky   Watery   Yeasty   Acidic   Sour   Clean   Earthy

Impressions that Change with Temperature/Time: _____

_____

What Worked? _____

_____

What Didn't Work? _____

What Changes Do I Want to Make? _____

_____

Overall Score (0–50) _____

Competition Notes (If you enter the beer in a competition, record the judges' impressions and scores.)

Competition Name: _____

Date: _____ Score: _____ Award: _____

Judge Notes: _____

_____

_____

_____

Competition Name: _____

Date: _____ Score: _____ Award: _____

Judge Notes: _____

_____

_____

_____

Competition Name: _____

Date: _____ Score: _____ Award: _____

Judge Notes: _____

_____

_____

_____

Competition Name: _____

Date: _____ Score: _____ Award: _____

Judge Notes: _____

_____

_____

_____

The Beer

Style: _____

Brew Type: ☐ Extract   ☐ Extract with Steeped Grains

            ☐ Partial Mash   ☐ All Grain

The Beer Story: _____

_____

_____

_____

_____

Desired Flavor and Aromas: _____

_____

_____

Gallons: _____ SRM (Color): _____

OG: _____ IBUs: _____

ABV: _____ Boil Time: _____

Ingredients

Malt/Grains/Sugar (if used)		
Amount	Ingredient	Brand

Extract (if used)		
Amount	Ingredient	Brand

Hops				
Amount	Variety	Type	AA %	Time in Boil

Type of Water: _____

Water: ☐ Bottled   ☐ Distilled/R.O.   ☐ Filtered

Water Salts: _____

Other Ingredients		
Amount	Ingredient	Add When?

The Recipe

Yeast: _____

_____

Starter Size: _____ Starter Gravity: _____ Days Fermented: _____

☐ Cold Crashed

Procedures

Mash Type: ☐ Steep   ☐ Single Infusion Mash
           ☐ Step Infusion Mash   ☐ Decoction

Mash Schedule			
Step	Target Temp	Rest Time	Infusion/Direct

Packaging

Dry Hop Schedule (if Dry Hopping)			
Amount	Variety	Temp	Days

Flavor Additions (e.g. vanilla, oak)	
Amount	Ingredient

Preparation

☐ Purchased all ingredients

☐ Equipment all accounted for

Total Cost: $ _____

Inventory Notes

_____
_____
_____
_____
_____
_____
_____
_____

Recipe Thoughts

Why choose the ingredients/techniques specified?

_____
_____
_____
_____
_____
_____
_____
_____
_____
_____
_____
_____
_____
_____

Brew Day

Date: _____

Brewer(s): _____

Time Started: _____

Temperature: _____

☐ Mash/Steep (if using grains)

Grain Crush: ☐ Coarse ☐ Medium ☐ Fine ☐ Flour

Ingredient Notes (Does the malt smell fresh? Firm or mushy?): _____

_____

Strike Water: Amount: _____ Temperature: _____

Mash/Steep Temperature(s): _____

Type of Sparge: ☐ Fly ☐ Batch ☐ No

Sparge Water: Amount: _____ Temperature: _____

First Runnings Gravity: _____

Final Runnings Gravity: _____

Notes: _____

_____

_____

Time Mash/Steep Completed: _____

☐ Boil

Boil Vessel: _____

Heat Source: ☐ Gas Stove   ☐ Electric Stove   ☐ Propane Burner

☐ Electric Heater   ☐ Other

Wort Collected: _____

Initial Boil Gravity: (*Stir the boil point vigorously for a minute to ensure even sugar mixing.*) _____

Time to Start Boil: _____

Time at Start of Boil: _____

Extract Added: ☐ Start of boil   ☐ Late: _____ minutes

☐ Scum Skimmed

Boil Notes (vigor, etc): _____

_____

Hops (as needed)

☐ _____ Minute Addition   ☐ _____ Minute Addition

☐ _____ Minute Addition   ☐ _____ Minute Addition

☐ _____ Minute Addition   ☐ _____ Minute Addition

☐ _____ Minute Addition

Notes: _____

_____

_____

☐ Adding Other Ingredients

Notes: _____

_____

_____

Time Boil Ended: _____

☐ Whirlpool

How Long?: _____

☐ Chill Wort

Cooling Mechanism: ☐ Closed Pot Overnight   ☐ Sink/Ice Bath

☐ Immersion Coil   ☐ Whirlpool Immersion   ☐ Counterflow Chiller

Chilling Start Time: _____

Water/Bath Temperature: _____

Temperature of Wort when Fully Chilled: _____

Chilling Finish Time: _____

☐ Hydrometer Reading:

    Original gravity (O.G.) _____

☐ Notes on pitching the yeast

_____

_____

_____

Temperature of the wort when the yeast is pitched: _____

☐ Used Starter

☐ Decanted Starter

Brew Day Finished: _____

Fermentation

Date: _____

Fermenter Type: ☐ Bucket   ☐ Glass Carboy   ☐ Plastic Carboy

                 ☐ Keg   ☐ Conical   ☐ Other: _____

Fermenter Closure: ☐ Airlock   ☐ Blow-off Tube   ☐ Foil Cap   ☐ Open

Length of Ferment: _____ Days

Aroma and Visual Notes: _____

_____

_____

_____

Ferment Temperature

Try to keep the temperature constant throughout the ferment.

Date: _____   Temp: _____

Date: _____   Temp: _____

Date: _____   Temp: _____

Date: _____   Temp: _____

Secondary Fermentation (if applicable)

Date: _____

Gravity at Transfer: _____

Length of Ferment: _____ Days

Aroma and Visual Notes: _____

_____

_____

_____

Additions to Secondary: _____

_____

_____

Finings/Clarification Aids: _____

_____

_____

Packaging

Date: _____

Hydrometer Reading: _____
(This number is the Final Gravity, or FG).

Calculate Alcohol by Volume (or ABV):

$$\underset{\text{Alcohol By Volume}}{\rule{3cm}{0.4pt}} = (\underset{\text{Original Gravity}}{\rule{3cm}{0.4pt}} - \underset{\text{Final Gravity}}{\rule{3cm}{0.4pt}}) / 7.5$$

Calculating Attenuation

$$\underset{\text{Apparent Attenuation}}{\rule{3cm}{0.4pt}} = 100 \times ((\underset{\text{Original Gravity}}{\rule{3cm}{0.4pt}} - \underset{\text{Final Gravity}}{\rule{3cm}{0.4pt}}) / \underset{\text{Original Gravity}}{\rule{3cm}{0.4pt}})$$

PACKAGE

☐ Bottle   ☐ Keg

CARBONATION

Desired Level of Carbonation: _____

☐ Primed

   with (sugar, wort, etc): _____

How much: _____

☐ Forced

Beer Temp: _____

CO_2 Setting: _____ p.s.i.

Method: ☐ Steady Pressure _____ week(s)

           ☐ Fast Carbonation: Shake at _____ p.s.i. for _____ minutes

Beer Storage Temperature: _____

The Final Beer

Chill and test a bottle. If carbonated, you're ready! Otherwise, wait another week and repeat. As you take notes, record how the beer changes as it warms up and lets off more CO_2.

Beer Temperature: _____

Pour Notes (carbonation, head, cloudy, etc.): _____
_____

Aroma Notes (What do you smell from the hops, the malt and the yeast?) _____
_____
_____

Appearance Notes (clarity, color, etc.)
_____
_____

Taste Notes (What tastes do you perceive from the ingredients?)
_____
_____

Mouth Feel/Finish
_____
_____

Overall Notes
_____
_____
_____

Circle all that apply

Bitter   Buttery   Cooked   Sweet   Hoppy   Fruity   Harsh   Malty   Metallic
Spicy   Roasted   Smoky   Watery   Yeasty   Acidic   Sour   Clean   Earthy

Impressions that Change with Temperature/Time: _____
_____

What Worked? _____
_____

What Didn't Work? _____

_____

What Changes Do I Want to Make? _____

_____

_____

Overall Score (0–50) _____

Competition Notes (If you enter the beer in a competition, record the judges' impressions and scores.)

Competition Name: _____

Date: _____ Score: _____ Award: _____

Judge Notes: _____

_____

_____

_____

Competition Name: _____

Date: _____ Score: _____ Award: _____

Judge Notes: _____

_____

_____

_____

Competition Name: _____

Date: _____ Score: _____ Award: _____

Judge Notes: _____

_____

_____

_____

Competition Name: _____

Date: _____ Score: _____ Award: _____

Judge Notes: _____

_____

_____

_____

The Beer

Style: _____

Brew Type: ☐ Extract   ☐ Extract with Steeped Grains
           ☐ Partial Mash   ☐ All Grain

The Beer Story: _____

_____

_____

_____

_____

Desired Flavor and Aromas: _____

_____

_____

Gallons: _____   SRM (Color): _____
OG: _____   IBUs: _____
ABV: _____   Boil Time: _____

Ingredients

Malt/Grains/Sugar (if used)		
Amount	Ingredient	Brand

Extract (if used)		
Amount	Ingredient	Brand

Hops				
Amount	Variety	Type	AA %	Time in Boil

Type of Water: _____

Water: ☐ Bottled   ☐ Distilled/R.O.   ☐ Filtered

Water Salts: _____

Other Ingredients		
Amount	Ingredient	Add When?

The Recipe

Yeast: _____

_____

Starter Size: _____ Starter Gravity: _____ Days Fermented: _____

☐ Cold Crashed

Procedures

Mash Type: ☐ Steep   ☐ Single Infusion Mash
            ☐ Step Infusion Mash ☐ Decoction

Mash Schedule			
Step	Target Temp	Rest Time	Infusion/Direct

Packaging

Dry Hop Schedule (if Dry Hopping)				
Amount	Variety		Temp	Days

Flavor Additions (e.g. vanilla, oak)	
Amount	Ingredient

Preparation

☐ Purchased all ingredients

☐ Equipment all accounted for

Total Cost: $ _____

Inventory Notes

_____

_____

_____

_____

_____

_____

_____

Recipe Thoughts

Why choose the ingredients/techniques specified?

_____

_____

_____

_____

_____

_____

_____

_____

_____

_____

_____

_____

_____

Brew Day

Date: _____

Brewer(s): _____

Time Started: _____

Temperature: _____

☐ Mash/Steep (if using grains)

Grain Crush: ☐ Coarse ☐ Medium ☐ Fine ☐ Flour

Ingredient Notes (Does the malt smell fresh? Firm or mushy?): _____

_____

Strike Water: Amount: _____ Temperature: _____

Mash/Steep Temperature(s): _____

Type of Sparge: ☐ Fly ☐ Batch ☐ No

Sparge Water: Amount: _____ Temperature: _____

First Runnings Gravity: _____

Final Runnings Gravity: _____

Notes: _____

_____

_____

Time Mash/Steep Completed: _____

☐ Boil

Boil Vessel: _____

Heat Source: ☐ Gas Stove   ☐ Electric Stove   ☐ Propane Burner

　　　　　　　☐ Electric Heater ☐ Other

Wort Collected: _____

Initial Boil Gravity: (*Stir the boil point vigorously for a minute to ensure even sugar mixing.*) _____

Time to Start Boil: _____

Time at Start of Boil: _____

Extract Added: ☐ Start of boil ☐ Late: _____ minutes

☐ Scum Skimmed

Boil Notes (vigor, etc): _____

_____

Hops (as needed)

☐ _____ Minute Addition   ☐ _____ Minute Addition

☐ _____ Minute Addition   ☐ _____ Minute Addition

☐ _____ Minute Addition   ☐ _____ Minute Addition

☐ _____ Minute Addition

Notes: _____

_____

_____

☐ Adding Other Ingredients

Notes: _____

_____

_____

Time Boil Ended: _____

☐ Whirlpool

How Long?: _____

☐ Chill Wort

Cooling Mechanism: ☐ Closed Pot Overnight   ☐ Sink/Ice Bath

☐ Immersion Coil   ☐ Whirlpool Immersion   ☐ Counterflow Chiller

Chilling Start Time: _____

Water/Bath Temperature: _____

Temperature of Wort when Fully Chilled: _____

Chilling Finish Time: _____

☐ Hydrometer Reading:

    Original gravity (O.G.) _____

☐ Notes on pitching the yeast

_____

_____

_____

Temperature of the wort when the yeast is pitched: _____

☐ Used Starter

☐ Decanted Starter

Brew Day Finished: _____

Fermentation

Date: _____

Fermenter Type: □ Bucket □ Glass Carboy □ Plastic Carboy

  □ Keg □ Conical □ Other: _____

Fermenter Closure: □ Airlock □ Blow-off Tube □ Foil Cap □ Open

Length of Ferment: _____ Days

Aroma and Visual Notes: _____

_____

_____

_____

Ferment Temperature

Try to keep the temperature constant throughout the ferment.

Date: _____ Temp: _____

Date: _____ Temp: _____

Date: _____ Temp: _____

Date: _____ Temp: _____

Secondary Fermentation (if applicable)

Date: _____

Gravity at Transfer: _____

Length of Ferment: _____ Days

Aroma and Visual Notes: _____

_____

_____

_____

Additions to Secondary: _____

_____

_____

Finings/Clarification Aids: _____

_____

_____

Packaging

Date: _____

Hydrometer Reading: _____
(This number is the Final Gravity, or FG).

Calculate Alcohol by Volume (or ABV):

$$\underset{\text{Alcohol By Volume}}{\underline{\hspace{3cm}}} = (\underset{\text{Original Gravity}}{\underline{\hspace{3cm}}} - \underset{\text{Final Gravity}}{\underline{\hspace{3cm}}}) / 7.5$$

Calculating Attenuation

$$\underset{\text{Apparent Attenuation}}{\underline{\hspace{3cm}}} = 100 \times ((\underset{\text{Original Gravity}}{\underline{\hspace{3cm}}} - \underset{\text{Final Gravity}}{\underline{\hspace{3cm}}}) / \underset{\text{Original Gravity}}{\underline{\hspace{3cm}}})$$

PACKAGE

☐ Bottle   ☐ Keg

CARBONATION

Desired Level of Carbonation: _____

☐ Primed

   with (sugar, wort, etc): _____

How much: _____

☐ Forced

Beer Temp: _____

CO_2 Setting: _____ p.s.i.

Method: ☐ Steady Pressure _____ week(s)

        ☐ Fast Carbonation: Shake at _____ p.s.i. for _____ minutes

Beer Storage Temperature: _____

The Final Beer

Chill and test a bottle. If carbonated, you're ready! Otherwise, wait another week and repeat. As you take notes, record how the beer changes as it warms up and lets off more CO_2.

Beer Temperature: _____

Pour Notes (carbonation, head, cloudy, etc.): _____

_____

Aroma Notes (What do you smell from the hops, the malt and the yeast?) _____

_____

_____

Appearance Notes (clarity, color, etc.)

_____

_____

Taste Notes (What tastes do you perceive from the ingredients?)

_____

_____

Mouth Feel/Finish

_____

_____

Overall Notes

_____

_____

_____

Circle all that apply

Bitter   Buttery   Cooked   Sweet   Hoppy   Fruity   Harsh   Malty   Metallic
Spicy   Roasted   Smoky   Watery   Yeasty   Acidic   Sour   Clean   Earthy

Impressions that Change with Temperature/Time: _____

_____

What Worked? _____

_____

What Didn't Work? _____

_____

What Changes Do I Want to Make? _____

_____

_____

Overall Score (0–50) _____

Competition Notes (If you enter the beer in a competition, record the judges' impressions and scores.)

Competition Name: _____

Date: _____ Score: _____ Award: _____

Judge Notes: _____

_____

_____

_____

Competition Name: _____

Date: _____ Score: _____ Award: _____

Judge Notes: _____

_____

_____

_____

Competition Name: _____

Date: _____ Score: _____ Award: _____

Judge Notes: _____

_____

_____

_____

Competition Name: _____

Date: _____ Score: _____ Award: _____

Judge Notes: _____

_____

_____

_____

The Beer

Style: _____

Brew Type: ☐ Extract   ☐ Extract with Steeped Grains
            ☐ Partial Mash   ☐ All Grain

The Beer Story: _____
_____
_____
_____
_____

Desired Flavor and Aromas: _____
_____
_____

Gallons: _____   SRM (Color): _____
OG: _____   IBUs: _____
ABV: _____   Boil Time: _____

Ingredients

Malt/Grains/Sugar (if used)		
Amount	Ingredient	Brand

Extract (if used)		
Amount	Ingredient	Brand

Hops				
Amount	Variety	Type	AA %	Time in Boil

Type of Water: _____

Water: ☐ Bottled   ☐ Distilled/R.O.   ☐ Filtered

Water Salts: _____

Other Ingredients		
Amount	Ingredient	Add When?

The Recipe

Yeast: _____

Starter Size: _____ Starter Gravity: _____ Days Fermented: _____

☐ Cold Crashed

Procedures

Mash Type: ☐ Steep ☐ Single Infusion Mash
            ☐ Step Infusion Mash ☐ Decoction

Mash Schedule			
Step	Target Temp	Rest Time	Infusion/Direct

Packaging

Dry Hop Schedule (if Dry Hopping)			
Amount	Variety	Temp	Days

Flavor Additions (e.g. vanilla, oak)	
Amount	Ingredient

Preparation

☐ Purchased all ingredients

☐ Equipment all accounted for

Total Cost: $ _____

Inventory Notes

_____

_____

_____

_____

_____

_____

_____

_____

Recipe Thoughts

Why choose the ingredients/techniques specified?

_____

_____

_____

_____

_____

_____

_____

_____

_____

_____

_____

_____

_____

Brew Day

Date: _____

Brewer(s): _____

Time Started: _____

Temperature: _____

☐ Mash/Steep (if using grains)

Grain Crush: ☐ Coarse ☐ Medium ☐ Fine ☐ Flour

Ingredient Notes (Does the malt smell fresh? Firm or mushy?): _____

_____

Strike Water: Amount: _____ Temperature: _____

Mash/Steep Temperature(s): _____

Type of Sparge: ☐ Fly ☐ Batch ☐ No

Sparge Water: Amount: _____ Temperature: _____

First Runnings Gravity: _____

Final Runnings Gravity: _____

Notes: _____

_____

_____

Time Mash/Steep Completed: _____

☐ Boil

Boil Vessel: _____

Heat Source: ☐ Gas Stove   ☐ Electric Stove   ☐ Propane Burner

                ☐ Electric Heater   ☐ Other

Wort Collected: _____

Initial Boil Gravity: (*Stir the boil point vigorously for a minute to ensure even*

sugar mixing.) _____

Time to Start Boil: _____

Time at Start of Boil: _____

Extract Added: ☐ Start of boil   ☐ Late: _____ minutes

☐ Scum Skimmed

Boil Notes (vigor, etc): _____

_____

Hops (as needed)

☐ _____ Minute Addition   ☐ _____ Minute Addition

☐ _____ Minute Addition   ☐ _____ Minute Addition

☐ _____ Minute Addition   ☐ _____ Minute Addition

☐ _____ Minute Addition

Notes: _____

_____

_____

☐ Adding Other Ingredients

Notes: _____

_____

_____

Time Boil Ended: _____

☐ Whirlpool

How Long?: _____

☐ Chill Wort

Cooling Mechanism: ☐ Closed Pot Overnight   ☐ Sink/Ice Bath

☐ Immersion Coil   ☐ Whirlpool Immersion   ☐ Counterflow Chiller

Chilling Start Time: _____

Water/Bath Temperature: _____

Temperature of Wort when Fully Chilled: _____

Chilling Finish Time: _____

☐ Hydrometer Reading:

    Original gravity (O.G.) _____

☐ Notes on pitching the yeast

_____

_____

_____

Temperature of the wort when the yeast is pitched: _____

☐ Used Starter

☐ Decanted Starter

Brew Day Finished: _____

Fermentation

Date: _____

Fermenter Type: ☐ Bucket   ☐ Glass Carboy   ☐ Plastic Carboy

             ☐ Keg   ☐ Conical   ☐ Other: _____

Fermenter Closure: ☐ Airlock   ☐ Blow-off Tube   ☐ Foil Cap   ☐ Open

Length of Ferment: _____ Days

Aroma and Visual Notes: _____

_____

_____

_____

Ferment Temperature

Try to keep the temperature constant throughout the ferment.

Date: _____ Temp: _____

Date: _____ Temp: _____

Date: _____ Temp: _____

Date: _____ Temp: _____

Secondary Fermentation (if applicable)

Date: _____

Gravity at Transfer: _____

Length of Ferment: _____ Days

Aroma and Visual Notes: _____

_____

_____

_____

Additions to Secondary: _____

_____

_____

Finings/Clarification Aids: _____

_____

_____

Packaging

Date: _____

Hydrometer Reading: _____
(This number is the Final Gravity, or FG).

Calculate Alcohol by Volume (or ABV):

$$\underset{\text{Alcohol By Volume}}{\underline{\hspace{3cm}}} = (\underset{\text{Original Gravity}}{\underline{\hspace{3cm}}} - \underset{\text{Final Gravity}}{\underline{\hspace{3cm}}}) \, / \, 7.5$$

Calculating Attenuation

$$\underset{\text{Apparent Attenuation}}{\underline{\hspace{3cm}}} = 100 \times ((\underset{\text{Original Gravity}}{\underline{\hspace{3cm}}} - \underset{\text{Final Gravity}}{\underline{\hspace{3cm}}}) \, / \, \underset{\text{Original Gravity}}{\underline{\hspace{3cm}}})$$

PACKAGE

☐ Bottle   ☐ Keg

CARBONATION

Desired Level of Carbonation: _____

☐ Primed

with (sugar, wort, etc): _____

How much: _____

☐ Forced

Beer Temp: _____

CO_2 Setting: _____ p.s.i.

Method: ☐ Steady Pressure _____ week(s)

☐ Fast Carbonation: Shake at _____ p.s.i. for _____ minutes

Beer Storage Temperature: _____

The Final Beer

Chill and test a bottle. If carbonated, you're ready! Otherwise, wait another week and repeat. As you take notes, record how the beer changes as it warms up and lets off more CO_2.

Beer Temperature: _____

Pour Notes (carbonation, head, cloudy, etc.): _____

_____

Aroma Notes (What do you smell from the hops, the malt and the yeast?) _____

_____

_____

Appearance Notes (clarity, color, etc.)

_____

_____

Taste Notes (What tastes do you perceive from the ingredients?)

_____

_____

Mouth Feel/Finish

_____

_____

Overall Notes

_____

_____

_____

Circle all that apply

Bitter   Buttery   Cooked   Sweet   Hoppy   Fruity   Harsh   Malty   Metallic
Spicy   Roasted   Smoky   Watery   Yeasty   Acidic   Sour   Clean   Earthy

Impressions that Change with Temperature/Time: _____

_____

What Worked? _____

_____

What Didn't Work? _____

_____

What Changes Do I Want to Make? _____

_____

_____

Overall Score (0–50) _____

Competition Notes (If you enter the beer in a competition, record the judges' impressions and scores.)

Competition Name: _____

Date: _____ Score: _____ Award: _____

Judge Notes: _____

_____

_____

_____

Competition Name: _____

Date: _____ Score: _____ Award: _____

Judge Notes: _____

_____

_____

_____

Competition Name: _____

Date: _____ Score: _____ Award: _____

Judge Notes: _____

_____

_____

_____

Competition Name: _____

Date: _____ Score: _____ Award: _____

Judge Notes: _____

_____

_____

_____

The Beer

Style: _____

Brew Type: ☐ Extract ☐ Extract with Steeped Grains
☐ Partial Mash ☐ All Grain

The Beer Story: _____

_____

_____

_____

_____

Desired Flavor and Aromas: _____

_____

_____

Gallons: _____ SRM (Color): _____
OG: _____ IBUs: _____
ABV: _____ Boil Time: _____

Ingredients

Malt/Grains/Sugar (if used)		
Amount	Ingredient	Brand

Extract (if used)

Amount	Ingredient	Brand

Hops

Amount	Variety	Type	AA %	Time in Boil

Type of Water: _____

Water: ☐ Bottled   ☐ Distilled/R.O.   ☐ Filtered

Water Salts: _____

Other Ingredients

Amount	Ingredient	Add When?

The Recipe

Yeast: _____

_____

Starter Size: _____ Starter Gravity: _____ Days Fermented: _____

☐ Cold Crashed

Procedures

Mash Type: ☐ Steep   ☐ Single Infusion Mash
              ☐ Step Infusion Mash   ☐ Decoction

Mash Schedule			
Step	Target Temp	Rest Time	Infusion/Direct

Packaging

Dry Hop Schedule (if Dry Hopping)			
Amount	Variety	Temp	Days

Flavor Additions (e.g. vanilla, oak)	
Amount	Ingredient

Preparation

☐ Purchased all ingredients

☐ Equipment all accounted for

Total Cost: $ _____

Inventory Notes

_____

_____

_____

_____

_____

_____

_____

Recipe Thoughts

Why choose the ingredients/techniques specified?

_____

_____

_____

_____

_____

_____

_____

_____

_____

_____

_____

_____

_____

Brew Day

Date: _____

Brewer(s): _____

Time Started: _____

Temperature: _____

☐ Mash/Steep (if using grains)

Grain Crush: ☐ Coarse   ☐ Medium   ☐ Fine   ☐ Flour

Ingredient Notes (Does the malt smell fresh? Firm or mushy?): _____

_____

Strike Water: Amount: _____   Temperature: _____

Mash/Steep Temperature(s): _____

Type of Sparge: ☐ Fly   ☐ Batch   ☐ No

Sparge Water: Amount: _____   Temperature: _____

First Runnings Gravity: _____

Final Runnings Gravity: _____

Notes: _____

_____

_____

Time Mash/Steep Completed: _____

☐ Boil

Boil Vessel: _____

Heat Source: ☐ Gas Stove   ☐ Electric Stove   ☐ Propane Burner

                ☐ Electric Heater   ☐ Other

Wort Collected: _____

Initial Boil Gravity: (*Stir the boil point vigorously for a minute to ensure even sugar mixing.*) _____

Time to Start Boil: _____

Time at Start of Boil: _____

Extract Added: ☐ Start of boil   ☐ Late: _____ minutes

☐ Scum Skimmed

Boil Notes (vigor, etc): _____

_____

Hops (as needed)

☐ _____ Minute Addition   ☐ _____ Minute Addition
☐ _____ Minute Addition   ☐ _____ Minute Addition
☐ _____ Minute Addition   ☐ _____ Minute Addition
☐ _____ Minute Addition

Notes: _____
_____
_____

☐ Adding Other Ingredients
Notes: _____
_____
_____

Time Boil Ended: _____
☐ Whirlpool
How Long?: _____
☐ Chill Wort
Cooling Mechanism: ☐ Closed Pot Overnight   ☐ Sink/Ice Bath
    ☐ Immersion Coil   ☐ Whirlpool Immersion   ☐ Counterflow Chiller
Chilling Start Time: _____
Water/Bath Temperature: _____
Temperature of Wort when Fully Chilled: _____
Chilling Finish Time: _____
☐ Hydrometer Reading:
    Original gravity (O.G.) _____
☐ Notes on pitching the yeast
_____
_____
_____

Temperature of the wort when the yeast is pitched: _____
☐ Used Starter
☐ Decanted Starter
Brew Day Finished: _____

Fermentation

Date: _____

Fermenter Type: ☐ Bucket   ☐ Glass Carboy   ☐ Plastic Carboy

              ☐ Keg   ☐ Conical   ☐ Other: _____

Fermenter Closure: ☐ Airlock   ☐ Blow-off Tube   ☐ Foil Cap   ☐ Open

Length of Ferment: _____ Days

Aroma and Visual Notes: _____

_____

_____

_____

Ferment Temperature

Try to keep the temperature constant throughout the ferment.

Date: _____   Temp: _____

Date: _____   Temp: _____

Date: _____   Temp: _____

Date: _____   Temp: _____

Secondary Fermentation (if applicable)

Date: _____

Gravity at Transfer: _____

Length of Ferment: _____ Days

Aroma and Visual Notes: _____

_____

_____

_____

Additions to Secondary: _____

_____

_____

Finings/Clarification Aids: _____

_____

_____

Packaging

Date: _____

Hydrometer Reading: _____
(This number is the Final Gravity, or FG).

Calculate Alcohol by Volume (or ABV):

$$\underset{\text{Alcohol By Volume}}{\rule{3cm}{0.4pt}} = (\underset{\text{Original Gravity}}{\rule{3cm}{0.4pt}} - \underset{\text{Final Gravity}}{\rule{3cm}{0.4pt}}) / 7.5$$

Calculating Attenuation

$$\underset{\text{Apparent Attenuation}}{\rule{3cm}{0.4pt}} = 100 \times ((\underset{\text{Original Gravity}}{\rule{3cm}{0.4pt}} - \underset{\text{Final Gravity}}{\rule{3cm}{0.4pt}}) / \underset{\text{Original Gravity}}{\rule{3cm}{0.4pt}})$$

PACKAGE

☐ Bottle   ☐ Keg

CARBONATION

Desired Level of Carbonation: _____

☐ Primed

    with (sugar, wort, etc): _____

How much: _____

☐ Forced

Beer Temp: _____

CO_2 Setting: _____ p.s.i.

Method: ☐ Steady Pressure _____ week(s)

        ☐ Fast Carbonation: Shake at _____ p.s.i. for _____ minutes

Beer Storage Temperature: _____

The Final Beer

Chill and test a bottle. If carbonated, you're ready! Otherwise, wait another week and repeat. As you take notes, record how the beer changes as it warms up and lets off more CO_2.

Beer Temperature: _____

Pour Notes (carbonation, head, cloudy, etc.): _____

_____

Aroma Notes (What do you smell from the hops, the malt and the yeast?) _____

_____

_____

Appearance Notes (clarity, color, etc.)

_____

_____

Taste Notes (What tastes do you perceive from the ingredients?)

_____

_____

Mouth Feel/Finish

_____

_____

Overall Notes

_____

_____

_____

Circle all that apply

Bitter   Buttery   Cooked   Sweet   Hoppy   Fruity   Harsh   Malty   Metallic

Spicy   Roasted   Smoky   Watery   Yeasty   Acidic   Sour   Clean   Earthy

Impressions that Change with Temperature/Time: _____

_____

What Worked? _____

_____

What Didn't Work? _____

What Changes Do I Want to Make? _____

_____

_____

Overall Score (0–50) _____

Competition Notes (If you enter the beer in a competition, record the judges' impressions and scores.)

Competition Name: _____

Date: _____ Score: _____ Award: _____

Judge Notes: _____

_____

_____

_____

Competition Name: _____

Date: _____ Score: _____ Award: _____

Judge Notes: _____

_____

_____

_____

Competition Name: _____

Date: _____ Score: _____ Award: _____

Judge Notes: _____

_____

_____

_____

Competition Name: _____

Date: _____ Score: _____ Award: _____

Judge Notes: _____

_____

_____

_____

The Beer

Style: _____

Brew Type: ☐ Extract   ☐ Extract with Steeped Grains

               ☐ Partial Mash   ☐ All Grain

The Beer Story: _____

_____

_____

_____

_____

Desired Flavor and Aromas: _____

_____

_____

Gallons: _____ SRM (Color): _____

OG: _____ IBUs: _____

ABV: _____ Boil Time: _____

Ingredients

Malt/Grains/Sugar (if used)		
Amount	Ingredient	Brand

Extract (if used)

Amount	Ingredient	Brand

Hops

Amount	Variety	Type	AA %	Time in Boil

Type of Water: _____

Water: ☐ Bottled   ☐ Distilled/R.O.   ☐ Filtered

Water Salts: _____

Other Ingredients

Amount	Ingredient	Add When?

The Recipe

Yeast: _____

_____

Starter Size: _____ Starter Gravity: _____ Days Fermented: _____

☐ Cold Crashed

Procedures

Mash Type: ☐ Steep   ☐ Single Infusion Mash
             ☐ Step Infusion Mash   ☐ Decoction

Mash Schedule			
Step	Target Temp	Rest Time	Infusion/Direct

Packaging

Dry Hop Schedule (if Dry Hopping)			
Amount	Variety	Temp	Days

Flavor Additions (e.g. vanilla, oak)	
Amount	Ingredient

Preparation

☐ Purchased all ingredients

☐ Equipment all accounted for

Total Cost: $ _____

Inventory Notes

_____

_____

_____

_____

_____

_____

_____

_____

Recipe Thoughts

Why choose the ingredients/techniques specified?

_____

_____

_____

_____

_____

_____

_____

_____

_____

_____

_____

_____

_____

_____

Brew Day

Date: _____

Brewer(s): _____

Time Started: _____

Temperature: _____

☐ Mash/Steep (if using grains)

Grain Crush: ☐ Coarse   ☐ Medium   ☐ Fine   ☐ Flour

Ingredient Notes (Does the malt smell fresh? Firm or mushy?): _____

_____

Strike Water: Amount: _____   Temperature: _____

Mash/Steep Temperature(s): _____

Type of Sparge: ☐ Fly   ☐ Batch   ☐ No

Sparge Water: Amount: _____   Temperature: _____

First Runnings Gravity: _____

Final Runnings Gravity: _____

Notes: _____

_____

_____

Time Mash/Steep Completed: _____

☐ Boil

Boil Vessel: _____

Heat Source: ☐ Gas Stove   ☐ Electric Stove   ☐ Propane Burner

☐ Electric Heater   ☐ Other

Wort Collected: _____

Initial Boil Gravity: (*Stir the boil point vigorously for a minute to ensure even sugar mixing.*) _____

Time to Start Boil: _____

Time at Start of Boil: _____

Extract Added: ☐ Start of boil   ☐ Late: _____ minutes

☐ Scum Skimmed

Boil Notes (vigor, etc): _____

Hops (as needed)

☐ _____ Minute Addition   ☐ _____ Minute Addition
☐ _____ Minute Addition   ☐ _____ Minute Addition
☐ _____ Minute Addition   ☐ _____ Minute Addition
☐ _____ Minute Addition

Notes: _____

_____

_____

☐ Adding Other Ingredients

Notes: _____

_____

_____

Time Boil Ended: _____

☐ Whirlpool

How Long?: _____

☐ Chill Wort

Cooling Mechanism: ☐ Closed Pot Overnight   ☐ Sink/Ice Bath
☐ Immersion Coil   ☐ Whirlpool Immersion   ☐ Counterflow Chiller

Chilling Start Time: _____

Water/Bath Temperature: _____

Temperature of Wort when Fully Chilled: _____

Chilling Finish Time: _____

☐ Hydrometer Reading:

   Original gravity (O.G.) _____

☐ Notes on pitching the yeast

_____

_____

_____

Temperature of the wort when the yeast is pitched: _____

☐ Used Starter

☐ Decanted Starter

Brew Day Finished: _____

Fermentation

Date: _____

Fermenter Type: ☐ Bucket   ☐ Glass Carboy   ☐ Plastic Carboy

              ☐ Keg   ☐ Conical   ☐ Other: _____

Fermenter Closure: ☐ Airlock   ☐ Blow-off Tube   ☐ Foil Cap   ☐ Open

Length of Ferment: _____ Days

Aroma and Visual Notes: _____

_____

_____

_____

Ferment Temperature

Try to keep the temperature constant throughout the ferment.

Date: _____ Temp: _____

Date: _____ Temp: _____

Date: _____ Temp: _____

Date: _____ Temp: _____

Secondary Fermentation (if applicable)

Date: _____

Gravity at Transfer: _____

Length of Ferment: _____ Days

Aroma and Visual Notes: _____

_____

_____

_____

Additions to Secondary: _____

_____

_____

Finings/Clarification Aids: _____

_____

_____

Packaging

Date: _____

Hydrometer Reading: _____
(This number is the Final Gravity, or FG).

Calculate Alcohol by Volume (or ABV):

$$\underset{\text{Alcohol By Volume}}{\underline{\hspace{3cm}}} = (\underset{\text{Original Gravity}}{\underline{\hspace{2.5cm}}} - \underset{\text{Final Gravity}}{\underline{\hspace{2.5cm}}}) / 7.5$$

Calculating Attenuation

$$\underset{\text{Apparent Attenuation}}{\underline{\hspace{3cm}}} = 100 \times ((\underset{\text{Original Gravity}}{\underline{\hspace{2.5cm}}} - \underset{\text{Final Gravity}}{\underline{\hspace{2.5cm}}}) / \underset{\text{Original Gravity}}{\underline{\hspace{2.5cm}}})$$

PACKAGE

☐ Bottle   ☐ Keg

CARBONATION

Desired Level of Carbonation: _____

☐ Primed

    with (sugar, wort, etc): _____

How much: _____

☐ Forced

Beer Temp: _____

CO_2 Setting: _____ p.s.i.

Method: ☐ Steady Pressure _____ week(s)

       ☐ Fast Carbonation: Shake at _____ p.s.i. for _____ minutes

Beer Storage Temperature: _____

The Final Beer

Chill and test a bottle. If carbonated, you're ready! Otherwise, wait another week and repeat. As you take notes, record how the beer changes as it warms up and lets off more CO_2.

Beer Temperature: _____

Pour Notes (carbonation, head, cloudy, etc.): _____

_____

Aroma Notes (What do you smell from the hops, the malt and the yeast?) _____

_____

_____

Appearance Notes (clarity, color, etc.)

_____

_____

Taste Notes (What tastes do you perceive from the ingredients?)

_____

_____

Mouth Feel/Finish

_____

_____

Overall Notes

_____

_____

_____

Circle all that apply

Bitter   Buttery   Cooked   Sweet   Hoppy   Fruity   Harsh   Malty   Metallic

Spicy   Roasted   Smoky   Watery   Yeasty   Acidic   Sour   Clean   Earthy

Impressions that Change with Temperature/Time: _____

_____

What Worked? _____

_____

What Didn't Work? _____

_____

What Changes Do I Want to Make? _____

_____

_____

Overall Score (0–50) _____

Competition Notes (If you enter the beer in a competition, record the judges' impressions and scores.)

Competition Name: _____

Date: _____ Score: _____ Award: _____

Judge Notes: _____

_____

_____

_____

Competition Name: _____

Date: _____ Score: _____ Award: _____

Judge Notes: _____

_____

_____

_____

Competition Name: _____

Date: _____ Score: _____ Award: _____

Judge Notes: _____

_____

_____

_____

Competition Name: _____

Date: _____ Score: _____ Award: _____

Judge Notes: _____

_____

_____

_____

The Beer

Style: _____

Brew Type: ☐ Extract   ☐ Extract with Steeped Grains

           ☐ Partial Mash   ☐ All Grain

The Beer Story: _____

_____

_____

_____

_____

Desired Flavor and Aromas: _____

_____

_____

Gallons: _____   SRM (Color): _____

OG: _____   IBUs: _____

ABV: _____   Boil Time: _____

Ingredients

Malt/Grains/Sugar (if used)		
Amount	Ingredient	Brand

Extract (if used)		
Amount	Ingredient	Brand

Hops				
Amount	Variety	Type	AA %	Time in Boil

Type of Water: _____

Water: ☐ Bottled   ☐ Distilled/R.O.   ☐ Filtered

Water Salts: _____

Other Ingredients		
Amount	Ingredient	Add When?

The Recipe

Yeast: _____

_____

Starter Size: _____ Starter Gravity: _____ Days Fermented: _____

☐ Cold Crashed

Procedures

Mash Type: ☐ Steep   ☐ Single Infusion Mash
           ☐ Step Infusion Mash   ☐ Decoction

Mash Schedule			
Step	Target Temp	Rest Time	Infusion/Direct

Packaging

Dry Hop Schedule (if Dry Hopping)			
Amount	Variety	Temp	Days

Flavor Additions (e.g. vanilla, oak)	
Amount	Ingredient

Preparation

☐ Purchased all ingredients

☐ Equipment all accounted for

Total Cost: $ _____

Inventory Notes

_____

_____

_____

_____

_____

_____

_____

_____

Recipe Thoughts

Why choose the ingredients/techniques specified?

_____

_____

_____

_____

_____

_____

_____

_____

_____

_____

_____

_____

_____

_____

Brew Day

Date: _____

Brewer(s): _____

Time Started: _____

Temperature: _____

☐ Mash/Steep (if using grains)

Grain Crush: ☐ Coarse   ☐ Medium   ☐ Fine   ☐ Flour

Ingredient Notes (Does the malt smell fresh? Firm or mushy?): _____

_____

Strike Water: Amount: _____   Temperature: _____

Mash/Steep Temperature(s): _____

Type of Sparge: ☐ Fly   ☐ Batch   ☐ No

Sparge Water: Amount: _____   Temperature: _____

First Runnings Gravity: _____

Final Runnings Gravity: _____

Notes: _____

_____

_____

Time Mash/Steep Completed: _____

☐ Boil

Boil Vessel: _____

Heat Source: ☐ Gas Stove   ☐ Electric Stove   ☐ Propane Burner

    ☐ Electric Heater   ☐ Other

Wort Collected: _____

Initial Boil Gravity: (*Stir the boil point vigorously for a minute to ensure even sugar mixing.*) _____

Time to Start Boil: _____

Time at Start of Boil: _____

Extract Added: ☐ Start of boil   ☐ Late: _____ minutes

☐ Scum Skimmed

Boil Notes (vigor, etc): _____

_____

Hops (as needed)

☐ _____ Minute Addition   ☐ _____ Minute Addition

☐ _____ Minute Addition   ☐ _____ Minute Addition

☐ _____ Minute Addition   ☐ _____ Minute Addition

☐ _____ Minute Addition

Notes: _____

_____

_____

☐ Adding Other Ingredients

Notes: _____

_____

_____

Time Boil Ended: _____

☐ Whirlpool

How Long?: _____

☐ Chill Wort

Cooling Mechanism: ☐ Closed Pot Overnight   ☐ Sink/Ice Bath

☐ Immersion Coil   ☐ Whirlpool Immersion   ☐ Counterflow Chiller

Chilling Start Time: _____

Water/Bath Temperature: _____

Temperature of Wort when Fully Chilled: _____

Chilling Finish Time: _____

☐ Hydrometer Reading:

    Original gravity (O.G.) _____

☐ Notes on pitching the yeast

_____

_____

Temperature of the wort when the yeast is pitched: _____

☐ Used Starter

☐ Decanted Starter

Brew Day Finished: _____

Fermentation

Date: _____

Fermenter Type: ☐ Bucket ☐ Glass Carboy ☐ Plastic Carboy
                 ☐ Keg   ☐ Conical   ☐ Other: _____

Fermenter Closure: ☐ Airlock ☐ Blow-off Tube ☐ Foil Cap ☐ Open

Length of Ferment: _____ Days

Aroma and Visual Notes: _____

_____

_____

_____

Ferment Temperature

Try to keep the temperature constant throughout the ferment.

Date: _____ Temp: _____

Date: _____ Temp: _____

Date: _____ Temp: _____

Date: _____ Temp: _____

Secondary Fermentation (if applicable)

Date: _____

Gravity at Transfer: _____

Length of Ferment: _____ Days

Aroma and Visual Notes: _____

_____

_____

_____

Additions to Secondary: _____

_____

_____

Finings/Clarification Aids: _____

_____

_____

Packaging

Date: _____

Hydrometer Reading: _____
(This number is the Final Gravity, or FG).

Calculate Alcohol by Volume (or ABV):

$$\underset{\text{Alcohol By Volume}}{\underline{\hspace{3cm}}} = (\underset{\text{Original Gravity}}{\underline{\hspace{3cm}}} - \underset{\text{Final Gravity}}{\underline{\hspace{3cm}}}) / 7.5$$

Calculating Attenuation

$$\underset{\text{Apparent Attenuation}}{\underline{\hspace{3cm}}} = 100 \times ((\underset{\text{Original Gravity}}{\underline{\hspace{3cm}}} - \underset{\text{Final Gravity}}{\underline{\hspace{3cm}}}) / \underset{\text{Original Gravity}}{\underline{\hspace{3cm}}})$$

PACKAGE

☐ Bottle   ☐ Keg

CARBONATION

Desired Level of Carbonation: _____

☐ Primed

  with (sugar, wort, etc): _____

How much: _____

☐ Forced

Beer Temp: _____

CO_2 Setting: _____ p.s.i.

Method: ☐ Steady Pressure _____ week(s)

          ☐ Fast Carbonation: Shake at _____ p.s.i. for _____ minutes

Beer Storage Temperature: _____

The Final Beer

Chill and test a bottle. If carbonated, you're ready! Otherwise, wait another week and repeat. As you take notes, record how the beer changes as it warms up and lets off more CO_2.

Beer Temperature: _____

Pour Notes (carbonation, head, cloudy, etc.): _____

_____

Aroma Notes (What do you smell from the hops, the malt and the yeast?) _____

_____

_____

Appearance Notes (clarity, color, etc.)

_____

_____

Taste Notes (What tastes do you perceive from the ingredients?)

_____

_____

Mouth Feel/Finish

_____

_____

Overall Notes

_____

_____

_____

Circle all that apply

Bitter   Buttery   Cooked   Sweet   Hoppy   Fruity   Harsh   Malty   Metallic
Spicy   Roasted   Smoky   Watery   Yeasty   Acidic   Sour   Clean   Earthy

Impressions that Change with Temperature/Time: _____

_____

What Worked? _____

_____

What Didn't Work? _____

_____

What Changes Do I Want to Make? _____

_____

_____

Overall Score (0–50) _____

Competition Notes (If you enter the beer in a competition, record the judges' impressions and scores.)

Competition Name: _____

Date: _____ Score: _____ Award: _____

Judge Notes: _____

_____

_____

_____

Competition Name: _____

Date: _____ Score: _____ Award: _____

Judge Notes: _____

_____

_____

_____

Competition Name: _____

Date: _____ Score: _____ Award: _____

Judge Notes: _____

_____

_____

_____

Competition Name: _____

Date: _____ Score: _____ Award: _____

Judge Notes: _____

_____

_____

_____

The Beer

Style: _____

Brew Type: ☐ Extract   ☐ Extract with Steeped Grains

           ☐ Partial Mash   ☐ All Grain

The Beer Story: _____

_____

_____

_____

_____

Desired Flavor and Aromas: _____

_____

_____

Gallons: _____   SRM (Color): _____

OG: _____   IBUs: _____

ABV: _____   Boil Time: _____

Ingredients

Malt/Grains/Sugar (if used)		
Amount	Ingredient	Brand

Extract (if used)

Amount	Ingredient	Brand

Hops

Amount	Variety	Type	AA %	Time in Boil

Type of Water: _____

Water: ☐ Bottled   ☐ Distilled/R.O.   ☐ Filtered

Water Salts: _____

Other Ingredients

Amount	Ingredient	Add When?

The Recipe

Yeast: _____

_____

Starter Size: _____ Starter Gravity: _____ Days Fermented: _____

☐ Cold Crashed

Procedures

Mash Type: ☐ Steep   ☐ Single Infusion Mash
              ☐ Step Infusion Mash   ☐ Decoction

Mash Schedule			
Step	Target Temp	Rest Time	Infusion/Direct

Packaging

Dry Hop Schedule (if Dry Hopping)			
Amount	Variety	Temp	Days

Flavor Additions (e.g. vanilla, oak)	
Amount	Ingredient

Preparation

☐ Purchased all ingredients

☐ Equipment all accounted for

Total Cost: $ _____

Inventory Notes

_____

_____

_____

_____

_____

_____

_____

_____

Recipe Thoughts

Why choose the ingredients/techniques specified?

_____

_____

_____

_____

_____

_____

_____

_____

_____

_____

_____

_____

_____

_____

_____

Brew Day

Date: _____

Brewer(s): _____

Time Started: _____

Temperature: _____

☐ Mash/Steep (if using grains)

Grain Crush: ☐ Coarse ☐ Medium ☐ Fine ☐ Flour

Ingredient Notes (Does the malt smell fresh? Firm or mushy?): _____

_____

Strike Water: Amount: _____ Temperature: _____

Mash/Steep Temperature(s): _____

Type of Sparge: ☐ Fly ☐ Batch ☐ No

Sparge Water: Amount: _____ Temperature: _____

First Runnings Gravity: _____

Final Runnings Gravity: _____

Notes: _____

_____

_____

Time Mash/Steep Completed: _____

☐ Boil

Boil Vessel: _____

Heat Source: ☐ Gas Stove ☐ Electric Stove ☐ Propane Burner
              ☐ Electric Heater ☐ Other

Wort Collected: _____

Initial Boil Gravity: (*Stir the boil point vigorously for a minute to ensure even sugar mixing.*) _____

Time to Start Boil: _____

Time at Start of Boil: _____

Extract Added: ☐ Start of boil ☐ Late: _____ minutes

☐ Scum Skimmed

Boil Notes (vigor, etc): _____

Hops (as needed)

☐ _____ Minute Addition   ☐ _____ Minute Addition

☐ _____ Minute Addition   ☐ _____ Minute Addition

☐ _____ Minute Addition   ☐ _____ Minute Addition

☐ _____ Minute Addition

Notes: _____

_____

_____

☐ Adding Other Ingredients

Notes: _____

_____

_____

Time Boil Ended: _____

☐ Whirlpool

How Long?: _____

☐ Chill Wort

Cooling Mechanism: ☐ Closed Pot Overnight   ☐ Sink/Ice Bath

☐ Immersion Coil   ☐ Whirlpool Immersion   ☐ Counterflow Chiller

Chilling Start Time: _____

Water/Bath Temperature: _____

Temperature of Wort when Fully Chilled: _____

Chilling Finish Time: _____

☐ Hydrometer Reading:

   Original gravity (O.G.) _____

☐ Notes on pitching the yeast

_____

_____

_____

Temperature of the wort when the yeast is pitched: _____

☐ Used Starter

☐ Decanted Starter

Brew Day Finished: _____

Fermentation

Date: _____

Fermenter Type: ☐ Bucket ☐ Glass Carboy ☐ Plastic Carboy
                 ☐ Keg   ☐ Conical   ☐ Other: _____
Fermenter Closure: ☐ Airlock ☐ Blow-off Tube ☐ Foil Cap ☐ Open
Length of Ferment: _____ Days
Aroma and Visual Notes: _____
_____
_____
_____

Ferment Temperature
Try to keep the temperature constant throughout the ferment.
Date: _____ Temp: _____
Date: _____ Temp: _____
Date: _____ Temp: _____
Date: _____ Temp: _____

Secondary Fermentation (if applicable)

Date: _____

Gravity at Transfer: _____
Length of Ferment: _____ Days
Aroma and Visual Notes: _____
_____
_____
_____

Additions to Secondary: _____
_____
_____

Finings/Clarification Aids: _____
_____
_____

Packaging

Date: _____

Hydrometer Reading: _____
(This number is the Final Gravity, or FG).

Calculate Alcohol by Volume (or ABV):

$$\underset{\text{Alcohol By Volume}}{\underline{\hspace{3cm}}} = (\underset{\text{Original Gravity}}{\underline{\hspace{2.5cm}}} - \underset{\text{Final Gravity}}{\underline{\hspace{2.5cm}}}) / 7.5$$

Calculating Attenuation

$$\underset{\text{Apparent Attenuation}}{\underline{\hspace{3cm}}} = 100 \times ((\underset{\text{Original Gravity}}{\underline{\hspace{2.5cm}}} - \underset{\text{Final Gravity}}{\underline{\hspace{2.5cm}}}) / \underset{\text{Original Gravity}}{\underline{\hspace{2.5cm}}})$$

PACKAGE

☐ Bottle　☐ Keg

CARBONATION

Desired Level of Carbonation: _____

☐ Primed

with (sugar, wort, etc): _____

How much: _____

☐ Forced

Beer Temp: _____

CO_2 Setting: _____p.s.i.

Method:　☐ Steady Pressure _____week(s)

　　　　☐ Fast Carbonation: Shake at _____p.s.i. for _____minutes

Beer Storage Temperature: _____

The Final Beer

Chill and test a bottle. If carbonated, you're ready! Otherwise, wait another week and repeat. As you take notes, record how the beer changes as it warms up and lets off more CO_2.

Beer Temperature: _____

Pour Notes (carbonation, head, cloudy, etc.): _____
_____

Aroma Notes (What do you smell from the hops, the malt and the yeast?) _____
_____
_____

Appearance Notes (clarity, color, etc.)
_____
_____

Taste Notes (What tastes do you perceive from the ingredients?)
_____
_____

Mouth Feel/Finish
_____
_____

Overall Notes
_____
_____
_____

Circle all that apply

Bitter   Buttery   Cooked   Sweet   Hoppy   Fruity   Harsh   Malty   Metallic
Spicy   Roasted   Smoky   Watery   Yeasty   Acidic   Sour   Clean   Earthy

Impressions that Change with Temperature/Time: _____
_____

What Worked? _____
_____

What Didn't Work? _____

_____

What Changes Do I Want to Make? _____

_____

_____

Overall Score (0–50) _____

Competition Notes (If you enter the beer in a competition, record the judges' impressions and scores.)

Competition Name: _____

Date: _____ Score: _____ Award: _____

Judge Notes: _____

_____

_____

_____

Competition Name: _____

Date: _____ Score: _____ Award: _____

Judge Notes: _____

_____

_____

_____

Competition Name: _____

Date: _____ Score: _____ Award: _____

Judge Notes: _____

_____

_____

_____

Competition Name: _____

Date: _____ Score: _____ Award: _____

Judge Notes: _____

_____

_____

_____

The Beer

Style: _____

Brew Type: ☐ Extract   ☐ Extract with Steeped Grains
            ☐ Partial Mash   ☐ All Grain

The Beer Story: _____

_____

_____

_____

_____

Desired Flavor and Aromas: _____

_____

_____

Gallons: _____   SRM (Color): _____

OG: _____   IBUs: _____

ABV: _____   Boil Time: _____

Ingredients

Malt/Grains/Sugar (if used)		
Amount	Ingredient	Brand

Extract (if used)

Amount	Ingredient	Brand

Hops

Amount	Variety	Type	AA %	Time in Boil

Type of Water: _____

Water: ☐ Bottled   ☐ Distilled/R.O.   ☐ Filtered

Water Salts: _____

Other Ingredients

Amount	Ingredient	Add When?

The Recipe

Yeast: _____

_____

Starter Size: _____ Starter Gravity: _____ Days Fermented: _____

☐ Cold Crashed

Procedures

Mash Type: ☐ Steep   ☐ Single Infusion Mash
            ☐ Step Infusion Mash   ☐ Decoction

Mash Schedule			
Step	Target Temp	Rest Time	Infusion/Direct

Packaging

Dry Hop Schedule (if Dry Hopping)			
Amount	Variety	Temp	Days

Flavor Additions (e.g. vanilla, oak)	
Amount	Ingredient

Preparation

☐ Purchased all ingredients

☐ Equipment all accounted for

Total Cost: $ _____

Inventory Notes

_____

_____

_____

_____

_____

_____

_____

_____

Recipe Thoughts

Why choose the ingredients/techniques specified?

_____

_____

_____

_____

_____

_____

_____

_____

_____

_____

_____

_____

_____

_____

Brew Day

Date: _____

Brewer(s): _____

Time Started: _____

Temperature: _____

☐ Mash/Steep (if using grains)

Grain Crush: ☐ Coarse   ☐ Medium   ☐ Fine   ☐ Flour

Ingredient Notes (Does the malt smell fresh? Firm or mushy?): _____

_____

Strike Water: Amount: _____   Temperature: _____

Mash/Steep Temperature(s): _____

Type of Sparge: ☐ Fly   ☐ Batch   ☐ No

Sparge Water: Amount: _____   Temperature: _____

First Runnings Gravity: _____

Final Runnings Gravity: _____

Notes: _____

_____

_____

Time Mash/Steep Completed: _____

☐ Boil

Boil Vessel: _____

Heat Source: ☐ Gas Stove   ☐ Electric Stove   ☐ Propane Burner

                      ☐ Electric Heater   ☐ Other

Wort Collected: _____

Initial Boil Gravity: (*Stir the boil point vigorously for a minute to ensure even*

sugar mixing.) _____

Time to Start Boil: _____

Time at Start of Boil: _____

Extract Added: ☐ Start of boil   ☐ Late: _____ minutes

☐ Scum Skimmed

Boil Notes (vigor, etc): _____

_____

Hops (as needed)

☐ _____ Minute Addition   ☐ _____ Minute Addition

☐ _____ Minute Addition   ☐ _____ Minute Addition

☐ _____ Minute Addition   ☐ _____ Minute Addition

☐ _____ Minute Addition

Notes: _____

_____

_____

☐ Adding Other Ingredients

Notes: _____

_____

_____

Time Boil Ended: _____

☐ Whirlpool

How Long?: _____

☐ Chill Wort

Cooling Mechanism: ☐ Closed Pot Overnight   ☐ Sink/Ice Bath

☐ Immersion Coil   ☐ Whirlpool Immersion   ☐ Counterflow Chiller

Chilling Start Time: _____

Water/Bath Temperature: _____

Temperature of Wort when Fully Chilled: _____

Chilling Finish Time: _____

☐ Hydrometer Reading:

    Original gravity (O.G.) _____

☐ Notes on pitching the yeast

_____

_____

_____

Temperature of the wort when the yeast is pitched: _____

☐ Used Starter

☐ Decanted Starter

Brew Day Finished: _____

Fermentation

Date: _____

Fermenter Type: ☐ Bucket   ☐ Glass Carboy   ☐ Plastic Carboy

☐ Keg   ☐ Conical   ☐ Other: _____

Fermenter Closure: ☐ Airlock   ☐ Blow-off Tube   ☐ Foil Cap   ☐ Open

Length of Ferment: _____ Days

Aroma and Visual Notes: _____

_____

_____

Ferment Temperature

Try to keep the temperature constant throughout the ferment.

Date: _____   Temp: _____

Date: _____   Temp: _____

Date: _____   Temp: _____

Date: _____   Temp: _____

Secondary Fermentation (if applicable)

Date: _____

Gravity at Transfer: _____

Length of Ferment: _____ Days

Aroma and Visual Notes: _____

_____

_____

Additions to Secondary: _____

_____

Finings/Clarification Aids: _____

_____

_____

Packaging

Date: _____

Hydrometer Reading: _____
(This number is the Final Gravity, or FG).

Calculate Alcohol by Volume (or ABV):

$$\underbrace{\rule{3cm}{0.4pt}}_{\text{Alcohol By Volume}} = (\underbrace{\rule{3cm}{0.4pt}}_{\text{Original Gravity}} - \underbrace{\rule{3cm}{0.4pt}}_{\text{Final Gravity}}) / 7.5$$

Calculating Attenuation

$$\underbrace{\rule{3cm}{0.4pt}}_{\text{Apparent Attenuation}} = 100 \times ((\underbrace{\rule{3cm}{0.4pt}}_{\text{Original Gravity}} - \underbrace{\rule{3cm}{0.4pt}}_{\text{Final Gravity}}) / \underbrace{\rule{3cm}{0.4pt}}_{\text{Original Gravity}})$$

PACKAGE

☐ Bottle   ☐ Keg

CARBONATION

Desired Level of Carbonation: _____

☐ Primed

    with (sugar, wort, etc): _____

How much: _____

☐ Forced

Beer Temp: _____

CO_2 Setting: _____ p.s.i.

Method: ☐ Steady Pressure _____ week(s)

        ☐ Fast Carbonation: Shake at _____ p.s.i. for _____ minutes

Beer Storage Temperature: _____

The Final Beer

Chill and test a bottle. If carbonated, you're ready! Otherwise, wait another week and repeat. As you take notes, record how the beer changes as it warms up and lets off more CO_2.

Beer Temperature: _____

Pour Notes (carbonation, head, cloudy, etc.): _____

_____

Aroma Notes (What do you smell from the hops, the malt and the yeast?) _____

_____

_____

Appearance Notes (clarity, color, etc.)

_____

_____

Taste Notes (What tastes do you perceive from the ingredients?)

_____

_____

Mouth Feel/Finish

_____

_____

Overall Notes

_____

_____

_____

Circle all that apply

Bitter   Buttery   Cooked   Sweet   Hoppy   Fruity   Harsh   Malty   Metallic

Spicy   Roasted   Smoky   Watery   Yeasty   Acidic   Sour   Clean   Earthy

Impressions that Change with Temperature/Time: _____

_____

What Worked? _____

_____

What Didn't Work? _____

_____

What Changes Do I Want to Make? _____

_____

_____

Overall Score (0–50) _____

Competition Notes (If you enter the beer in a competition, record the judges' impressions and scores.)

Competition Name: _____

Date: _____ Score: _____ Award: _____

Judge Notes: _____

_____

_____

_____

Competition Name: _____

Date: _____ Score: _____ Award: _____

Judge Notes: _____

_____

_____

_____

Competition Name: _____

Date: _____ Score: _____ Award: _____

Judge Notes: _____

_____

_____

_____

Competition Name: _____

Date: _____ Score: _____ Award: _____

Judge Notes: _____

_____

_____

_____

The Beer

Style: _____

Brew Type: ☐ Extract   ☐ Extract with Steeped Grains
            ☐ Partial Mash   ☐ All Grain

The Beer Story: _____
_____
_____
_____
_____

Desired Flavor and Aromas: _____
_____
_____

Gallons: _____   SRM (Color): _____
OG: _____   IBUs: _____
ABV: _____   Boil Time: _____

Ingredients

Malt/Grains/Sugar (if used)		
Amount	Ingredient	Brand

Extract (if used)

Amount	Ingredient	Brand

Hops

Amount	Variety	Type	AA %	Time in Boil

Type of Water: _____

Water: ☐ Bottled   ☐ Distilled/R.O.   ☐ Filtered

Water Salts: _____

Other Ingredients

Amount	Ingredient	Add When?

The Recipe

Yeast: _____

_____

Starter Size: _____ Starter Gravity: _____ Days Fermented: _____

☐ Cold Crashed

Procedures

Mash Type: ☐ Steep   ☐ Single Infusion Mash
           ☐ Step Infusion Mash ☐ Decoction

Mash Schedule			
Step	Target Temp	Rest Time	Infusion/Direct

Packaging

Dry Hop Schedule (if Dry Hopping)			
Amount	Variety	Temp	Days

Flavor Additions (e.g. vanilla, oak)	
Amount	Ingredient

Preparation

☐ Purchased all ingredients

☐ Equipment all accounted for

Total Cost: $ _____

Inventory Notes

_____

_____

_____

_____

_____

_____

_____

_____

Recipe Thoughts

Why choose the ingredients/techniques specified?

_____

_____

_____

_____

_____

_____

_____

_____

_____

_____

_____

_____

_____

_____

Brew Day

Date: _____

Brewer(s): _____

Time Started: _____

Temperature: _____

☐ Mash/Steep (if using grains)

Grain Crush: ☐ Coarse   ☐ Medium   ☐ Fine   ☐ Flour

Ingredient Notes (Does the malt smell fresh? Firm or mushy?): _____

_____

Strike Water: Amount: _____   Temperature: _____

Mash/Steep Temperature(s): _____

Type of Sparge: ☐ Fly   ☐ Batch   ☐ No

Sparge Water: Amount: _____   Temperature: _____

First Runnings Gravity: _____

Final Runnings Gravity: _____

Notes: _____

_____

_____

Time Mash/Steep Completed: _____

☐ Boil

Boil Vessel: _____

Heat Source: ☐ Gas Stove   ☐ Electric Stove   ☐ Propane Burner

                ☐ Electric Heater   ☐ Other

Wort Collected: _____

Initial Boil Gravity: (*Stir the boil point vigorously for a minute to ensure even sugar mixing.*) _____

Time to Start Boil: _____

Time at Start of Boil: _____

Extract Added: ☐ Start of boil   ☐ Late: _____ minutes

☐ Scum Skimmed

Boil Notes (vigor, etc): _____

_____

Hops (as needed)

☐ _____ Minute Addition   ☐ _____ Minute Addition
☐ _____ Minute Addition   ☐ _____ Minute Addition
☐ _____ Minute Addition   ☐ _____ Minute Addition
☐ _____ Minute Addition

Notes: _____
_____
_____

☐ Adding Other Ingredients

Notes: _____
_____
_____

Time Boil Ended: _____
☐ Whirlpool
How Long?: _____
☐ Chill Wort
Cooling Mechanism: ☐ Closed Pot Overnight   ☐ Sink/Ice Bath
☐ Immersion Coil   ☐ Whirlpool Immersion   ☐ Counterflow Chiller
Chilling Start Time: _____
Water/Bath Temperature: _____
Temperature of Wort when Fully Chilled: _____
Chilling Finish Time: _____
☐ Hydrometer Reading:
    Original gravity (O.G.) _____
☐ Notes on pitching the yeast
_____
_____
_____

Temperature of the wort when the yeast is pitched: _____
☐ Used Starter
☐ Decanted Starter
Brew Day Finished: _____

Fermentation

Date: _____

Fermenter Type: ☐ Bucket   ☐ Glass Carboy   ☐ Plastic Carboy
                ☐ Keg   ☐ Conical   ☐ Other: _____

Fermenter Closure: ☐ Airlock   ☐ Blow-off Tube   ☐ Foil Cap   ☐ Open

Length of Ferment: _____ Days

Aroma and Visual Notes: _____

_____

_____

_____

Ferment Temperature

Try to keep the temperature constant throughout the ferment.

Date: _____ Temp: _____

Date: _____ Temp: _____

Date: _____ Temp: _____

Date: _____ Temp: _____

Secondary Fermentation (if applicable)

Date: _____

Gravity at Transfer: _____

Length of Ferment: _____ Days

Aroma and Visual Notes: _____

_____

_____

_____

Additions to Secondary: _____

_____

_____

Finings/Clarification Aids: _____

_____

_____

Packaging

Date: _____

Hydrometer Reading: _____
(This number is the Final Gravity, or FG).

Calculate Alcohol by Volume (or ABV):

$$\underset{\text{Alcohol By Volume}}{\underline{\hspace{3cm}}} = (\underset{\text{Original Gravity}}{\underline{\hspace{3cm}}} - \underset{\text{Final Gravity}}{\underline{\hspace{3cm}}}) / 7.5$$

Calculating Attenuation

$$\underset{\text{Apparent Attenuation}}{\underline{\hspace{3cm}}} = 100 \times ((\underset{\text{Original Gravity}}{\underline{\hspace{3cm}}} - \underset{\text{Final Gravity}}{\underline{\hspace{3cm}}}) / \underset{\text{Original Gravity}}{\underline{\hspace{3cm}}})$$

PACKAGE

☐ Bottle   ☐ Keg

CARBONATION

Desired Level of Carbonation: _____

☐ Primed

    with (sugar, wort, etc): _____

How much: _____

☐ Forced

Beer Temp: _____

CO_2 Setting: _____ p.s.i.

Method: ☐ Steady Pressure _____ week(s)

       ☐ Fast Carbonation: Shake at _____ p.s.i. for _____ minutes

Beer Storage Temperature: _____

The Final Beer

Chill and test a bottle. If carbonated, you're ready! Otherwise, wait another week and repeat. As you take notes, record how the beer changes as it warms up and lets off more CO_2.

Beer Temperature: _____

Pour Notes (carbonation, head, cloudy, etc.): _____

_____

Aroma Notes (What do you smell from the hops, the malt and the yeast?) _____

_____

_____

Appearance Notes (clarity, color, etc.)

_____

_____

Taste Notes (What tastes do you perceive from the ingredients?)

_____

_____

Mouth Feel/Finish

_____

_____

Overall Notes

_____

_____

_____

Circle all that apply

Bitter   Buttery   Cooked   Sweet   Hoppy   Fruity   Harsh   Malty   Metallic
Spicy   Roasted   Smoky   Watery   Yeasty   Acidic   Sour   Clean   Earthy

Impressions that Change with Temperature/Time: _____

_____

What Worked? _____

_____

What Didn't Work? _____

_____

What Changes Do I Want to Make? _____

_____

_____

Overall Score (0–50) _____

Competition Notes (If you enter the beer in a competition, record the judges' impressions and scores.)

Competition Name: _____

Date: _____ Score: _____ Award: _____

Judge Notes: _____

_____

_____

_____

Competition Name: _____

Date: _____ Score: _____ Award: _____

Judge Notes: _____

_____

_____

_____

Competition Name: _____

Date: _____ Score: _____ Award: _____

Judge Notes: _____

_____

_____

_____

Competition Name: _____

Date: _____ Score: _____ Award: _____

Judge Notes: _____

_____

_____

_____

The Beer

Style: _____

Brew Type: ☐ Extract   ☐ Extract with Steeped Grains
            ☐ Partial Mash   ☐ All Grain

The Beer Story: _____
_____
_____
_____

Desired Flavor and Aromas: _____
_____
_____

Gallons: _____   SRM (Color): _____
OG: _____   IBUs: _____
ABV: _____   Boil Time: _____

Ingredients

Malt/Grains/Sugar (if used)		
Amount	Ingredient	Brand

Extract (if used)

Amount	Ingredient	Brand

Hops

Amount	Variety	Type	AA %	Time in Boil

Type of Water: _____

Water: ☐ Bottled ☐ Distilled/R.O. ☐ Filtered

Water Salts: _____

Other Ingredients

Amount	Ingredient	Add When?

The Recipe

Yeast: _____

_____

Starter Size: _____ Starter Gravity: _____ Days Fermented: _____

☐ Cold Crashed

Procedures

Mash Type: ☐ Steep   ☐ Single Infusion Mash
             ☐ Step Infusion Mash   ☐ Decoction

Mash Schedule			
Step	Target Temp	Rest Time	Infusion/Direct

Packaging

Dry Hop Schedule (if Dry Hopping)			
Amount	Variety	Temp	Days

Flavor Additions (e.g. vanilla, oak)	
Amount	Ingredient

Preparation

☐ Purchased all ingredients

☐ Equipment all accounted for

Total Cost: $ _____

Inventory Notes

_____

_____

_____

_____

_____

_____

_____

_____

Recipe Thoughts

Why choose the ingredients/techniques specified?

_____

_____

_____

_____

_____

_____

_____

_____

_____

_____

_____

_____

_____

_____

Brew Day

Date: _____

Brewer(s): _____

Time Started: _____

Temperature: _____

☐ **Mash/Steep (if using grains)**

Grain Crush: ☐ Coarse   ☐ Medium   ☐ Fine   ☐ Flour

Ingredient Notes (Does the malt smell fresh? Firm or mushy?): _____

_____

Strike Water: Amount: _____   Temperature: _____

Mash/Steep Temperature(s): _____

Type of Sparge: ☐ Fly   ☐ Batch   ☐ No

Sparge Water: Amount: _____   Temperature: _____

First Runnings Gravity: _____

Final Runnings Gravity: _____

Notes: _____

_____

_____

Time Mash/Steep Completed: _____

☐ **Boil**

Boil Vessel: _____

Heat Source: ☐ Gas Stove   ☐ Electric Stove   ☐ Propane Burner

   ☐ Electric Heater   ☐ Other

Wort Collected: _____

Initial Boil Gravity: (*Stir the boil point vigorously for a minute to ensure even sugar mixing.*) _____

Time to Start Boil: _____

Time at Start of Boil: _____

Extract Added: ☐ Start of boil   ☐ Late: _____ minutes

☐ Scum Skimmed

Boil Notes (vigor, etc): _____

Hops (as needed)

☐ _____ Minute Addition   ☐ _____ Minute Addition

☐ _____ Minute Addition   ☐ _____ Minute Addition

☐ _____ Minute Addition   ☐ _____ Minute Addition

☐ _____ Minute Addition

Notes: _____

_____

_____

☐ Adding Other Ingredients

Notes: _____

_____

_____

Time Boil Ended: _____

☐ Whirlpool

How Long?: _____

☐ Chill Wort

Cooling Mechanism: ☐ Closed Pot Overnight   ☐ Sink/Ice Bath

☐ Immersion Coil   ☐ Whirlpool Immersion   ☐ Counterflow Chiller

Chilling Start Time: _____

Water/Bath Temperature: _____

Temperature of Wort when Fully Chilled: _____

Chilling Finish Time: _____

☐ Hydrometer Reading:

   Original gravity (O.G.) _____

☐ Notes on pitching the yeast

_____

_____

_____

Temperature of the wort when the yeast is pitched: _____

☐ Used Starter

☐ Decanted Starter

Brew Day Finished: _____

Fermentation

Date: _____

Fermenter Type: ☐ Bucket ☐ Glass Carboy ☐ Plastic Carboy
☐ Keg ☐ Conical ☐ Other: _____

Fermenter Closure: ☐ Airlock ☐ Blow-off Tube ☐ Foil Cap ☐ Open

Length of Ferment: _____ Days

Aroma and Visual Notes: _____

_____

_____

_____

Ferment Temperature

Try to keep the temperature constant throughout the ferment.

Date: _____ Temp: _____

Date: _____ Temp: _____

Date: _____ Temp: _____

Date: _____ Temp: _____

Secondary Fermentation (if applicable)

Date: _____

Gravity at Transfer: _____

Length of Ferment: _____ Days

Aroma and Visual Notes: _____

_____

_____

_____

Additions to Secondary: _____

_____

_____

Finings/Clarification Aids: _____

_____

_____

Packaging

Date: _____

Hydrometer Reading: _____
(This number is the Final Gravity, or FG).

Calculate Alcohol by Volume (or ABV):

$$\underset{\text{Alcohol By Volume}}{\underline{\hspace{3cm}}} = (\underset{\text{Original Gravity}}{\underline{\hspace{3cm}}} - \underset{\text{Final Gravity}}{\underline{\hspace{3cm}}}) / 7.5$$

Calculating Attenuation

$$\underset{\text{Apparent Attenuation}}{\underline{\hspace{3cm}}} = 100 \times ((\underset{\text{Original Gravity}}{\underline{\hspace{3cm}}} - \underset{\text{Final Gravity}}{\underline{\hspace{3cm}}}) / \underset{\text{Original Gravity}}{\underline{\hspace{3cm}}})$$

PACKAGE

☐ Bottle   ☐ Keg

CARBONATION

Desired Level of Carbonation: _____

☐ Primed

with (sugar, wort, etc): _____

How much: _____

☐ Forced

Beer Temp: _____

CO_2 Setting: _____ p.s.i.

Method: ☐ Steady Pressure _____ week(s)

☐ Fast Carbonation: Shake at _____ p.s.i. for _____ minutes

Beer Storage Temperature: _____

The Final Beer

Chill and test a bottle. If carbonated, you're ready! Otherwise, wait another week and repeat. As you take notes, record how the beer changes as it warms up and lets off more CO_2.

Beer Temperature: _____

Pour Notes (carbonation, head, cloudy, etc.): _____

_____

Aroma Notes (What do you smell from the hops, the malt and the yeast?) _____

_____

_____

Appearance Notes (clarity, color, etc.)

_____

_____

Taste Notes (What tastes do you perceive from the ingredients?)

_____

_____

Mouth Feel/Finish

_____

_____

Overall Notes

_____

_____

_____

Circle all that apply

Bitter   Buttery   Cooked   Sweet   Hoppy   Fruity   Harsh   Malty   Metallic

Spicy   Roasted   Smoky   Watery   Yeasty   Acidic   Sour   Clean   Earthy

Impressions that Change with Temperature/Time: _____

_____

What Worked? _____

_____

What Didn't Work? _____

_____

What Changes Do I Want to Make? _____

_____

Overall Score (0–50) _____

Competition Notes (If you enter the beer in a competition, record the judges' impressions and scores.)

Competition Name: _____

Date: _____ Score: _____ Award: _____

Judge Notes: _____

_____

_____

_____

Competition Name: _____

Date: _____ Score: _____ Award: _____

Judge Notes: _____

_____

_____

_____

Competition Name: _____

Date: _____ Score: _____ Award: _____

Judge Notes: _____

_____

_____

_____

Competition Name: _____

Date: _____ Score: _____ Award: _____

Judge Notes: _____

_____

_____

_____

The Beer

Style: _____

Brew Type: ☐ Extract   ☐ Extract with Steeped Grains
           ☐ Partial Mash   ☐ All Grain

The Beer Story: _____
_____
_____
_____
_____

Desired Flavor and Aromas: _____
_____
_____

Gallons: _____   SRM (Color): _____
OG: _____   IBUs: _____
ABV: _____   Boil Time: _____

Ingredients

Malt/Grains/Sugar (if used)		
Amount	Ingredient	Brand

Extract (if used)		
Amount	Ingredient	Brand

Hops				
Amount	Variety	Type	AA %	Time in Boil

Type of Water: _____

Water: ☐ Bottled   ☐ Distilled/R.O.   ☐ Filtered

Water Salts: _____

Other Ingredients		
Amount	Ingredient	Add When?

The Recipe

Yeast: _____

_____

Starter Size: _____ Starter Gravity: _____ Days Fermented: _____

☐ Cold Crashed

Procedures

Mash Type: ☐ Steep   ☐ Single Infusion Mash
           ☐ Step Infusion Mash   ☐ Decoction

Mash Schedule			
Step	Target Temp	Rest Time	Infusion/Direct

Packaging

Dry Hop Schedule (if Dry Hopping)			
Amount	Variety	Temp	Days

Flavor Additions (e.g. vanilla, oak)	
Amount	Ingredient

Preparation

☐ Purchased all ingredients

☐ Equipment all accounted for

Total Cost: $ _____

Inventory Notes

_____

_____

_____

_____

_____

_____

_____

_____

Recipe Thoughts

Why choose the ingredients/techniques specified?

_____

_____

_____

_____

_____

_____

_____

_____

_____

_____

_____

_____

_____

_____

Brew Day

Date: _____

Brewer(s): _____

Time Started: _____

Temperature: _____

☐ Mash/Steep (if using grains)

Grain Crush: ☐ Coarse   ☐ Medium   ☐ Fine   ☐ Flour

Ingredient Notes (Does the malt smell fresh? Firm or mushy?): _____

_____

Strike Water: Amount: _____   Temperature: _____

Mash/Steep Temperature(s): _____

Type of Sparge: ☐ Fly   ☐ Batch   ☐ No

Sparge Water: Amount: _____   Temperature: _____

First Runnings Gravity: _____

Final Runnings Gravity: _____

Notes: _____

_____

_____

Time Mash/Steep Completed: _____

☐ Boil

Boil Vessel: _____

Heat Source: ☐ Gas Stove   ☐ Electric Stove   ☐ Propane Burner

   ☐ Electric Heater   ☐ Other

Wort Collected: _____

Initial Boil Gravity: (*Stir the boil point vigorously for a minute to ensure even sugar mixing.*) _____

Time to Start Boil: _____

Time at Start of Boil: _____

Extract Added: ☐ Start of boil   ☐ Late: _____ minutes

☐ Scum Skimmed

Boil Notes (vigor, etc): _____

_____

Hops (as needed)

☐ _____ Minute Addition   ☐ _____ Minute Addition

☐ _____ Minute Addition   ☐ _____ Minute Addition

☐ _____ Minute Addition   ☐ _____ Minute Addition

☐ _____ Minute Addition

Notes: _____

_____

_____

☐ Adding Other Ingredients

Notes: _____

_____

_____

Time Boil Ended: _____

☐ Whirlpool

How Long?: _____

☐ Chill Wort

Cooling Mechanism: ☐ Closed Pot Overnight   ☐ Sink/Ice Bath

☐ Immersion Coil   ☐ Whirlpool Immersion   ☐ Counterflow Chiller

Chilling Start Time: _____

Water/Bath Temperature: _____

Temperature of Wort when Fully Chilled: _____

Chilling Finish Time: _____

☐ Hydrometer Reading:

    Original gravity (O.G.) _____

☐ Notes on pitching the yeast

_____

_____

_____

Temperature of the wort when the yeast is pitched: _____

☐ Used Starter

☐ Decanted Starter

Brew Day Finished: _____

Fermentation

Date: _____

Fermenter Type: ☐ Bucket   ☐ Glass Carboy   ☐ Plastic Carboy

                ☐ Keg   ☐ Conical   ☐ Other: _____

Fermenter Closure: ☐ Airlock   ☐ Blow-off Tube   ☐ Foil Cap   ☐ Open

Length of Ferment: _____ Days

Aroma and Visual Notes: _____

_____

_____

_____

Ferment Temperature

Try to keep the temperature constant throughout the ferment.

Date: _____ Temp: _____

Date: _____ Temp: _____

Date: _____ Temp: _____

Date: _____ Temp: _____

Secondary Fermentation (if applicable)

Date: _____

Gravity at Transfer: _____

Length of Ferment: _____ Days

Aroma and Visual Notes: _____

_____

_____

_____

Additions to Secondary: _____

_____

_____

Finings/Clarification Aids: _____

_____

_____

Packaging

Date: _____

Hydrometer Reading: _____
(This number is the Final Gravity, or FG).

Calculate Alcohol by Volume (or ABV):

$$\underset{\text{Alcohol By Volume}}{\underline{\hspace{3cm}}} = (\underset{\text{Original Gravity}}{\underline{\hspace{3cm}}} - \underset{\text{Final Gravity}}{\underline{\hspace{3cm}}}) / 7.5$$

Calculating Attenuation

$$\underset{\text{Apparent Attenuation}}{\underline{\hspace{3cm}}} = 100 \times ((\underset{\text{Original Gravity}}{\underline{\hspace{3cm}}} - \underset{\text{Final Gravity}}{\underline{\hspace{3cm}}}) / \underset{\text{Original Gravity}}{\underline{\hspace{3cm}}})$$

PACKAGE

☐ Bottle   ☐ Keg

CARBONATION

Desired Level of Carbonation: _____

☐ Primed

    with (sugar, wort, etc): _____

How much: _____

☐ Forced

Beer Temp: _____

CO_2 Setting: _____ p.s.i.

Method: ☐ Steady Pressure _____ week(s)

        ☐ Fast Carbonation: Shake at _____ p.s.i. for _____ minutes

Beer Storage Temperature: _____

The Final Beer

Chill and test a bottle. If carbonated, you're ready! Otherwise, wait another week and repeat. As you take notes, record how the beer changes as it warms up and lets off more CO_2.

Beer Temperature: _____

Pour Notes (carbonation, head, cloudy, etc.): _____

Aroma Notes (What do you smell from the hops, the malt and the yeast?) _____

_____

Appearance Notes (clarity, color, etc.)

_____

Taste Notes (What tastes do you perceive from the ingredients?)

_____

Mouth Feel/Finish

_____

Overall Notes

_____

Circle all that apply

Bitter   Buttery   Cooked   Sweet   Hoppy   Fruity   Harsh   Malty   Metallic
Spicy   Roasted   Smoky   Watery   Yeasty   Acidic   Sour   Clean   Earthy

Impressions that Change with Temperature/Time: _____

_____

What Worked? _____

_____

What Didn't Work? _____

_____

What Changes Do I Want to Make? _____

_____

_____

Overall Score (0–50) _____

Competition Notes (If you enter the beer in a competition, record the judges' impressions and scores.)

Competition Name: _____

Date: _____ Score: _____ Award: _____

Judge Notes: _____

_____

_____

_____

Competition Name: _____

Date: _____ Score: _____ Award: _____

Judge Notes: _____

_____

_____

_____

Competition Name: _____

Date: _____ Score: _____ Award: _____

Judge Notes: _____

_____

_____

_____

Competition Name: _____

Date: _____ Score: _____ Award: _____

Judge Notes: _____

_____

_____

_____

The Beer

Style: _____

Brew Type: ☐ Extract   ☐ Extract with Steeped Grains
            ☐ Partial Mash   ☐ All Grain

The Beer Story: _____
_____
_____
_____
_____

Desired Flavor and Aromas: _____
_____
_____

Gallons: _____   SRM (Color): _____
OG: _____   IBUs: _____
ABV: _____   Boil Time: _____

Ingredients

Malt/Grains/Sugar (if used)		
Amount	Ingredient	Brand

Extract (if used)

Amount	Ingredient	Brand

Hops

Amount	Variety	Type	AA %	Time in Boil

Type of Water: _____

Water: ☐ Bottled   ☐ Distilled/R.O.   ☐ Filtered

Water Salts: _____

Other Ingredients

Amount	Ingredient	Add When?

The Recipe

Yeast: _____

_____

Starter Size: _____ Starter Gravity: _____ Days Fermented: _____

☐ Cold Crashed

Procedures

Mash Type: ☐ Steep   ☐ Single Infusion Mash
            ☐ Step Infusion Mash   ☐ Decoction

Mash Schedule			
Step	Target Temp	Rest Time	Infusion/Direct

Packaging

Dry Hop Schedule (if Dry Hopping)			
Amount	Variety	Temp	Days

Flavor Additions (e.g. vanilla, oak)	
Amount	Ingredient

Preparation

☐ Purchased all ingredients

☐ Equipment all accounted for

Total Cost: $ _____

Inventory Notes

_____
_____
_____
_____
_____
_____
_____

Recipe Thoughts

Why choose the ingredients/techniques specified?

_____
_____
_____
_____
_____
_____
_____
_____
_____
_____
_____
_____
_____
_____

Brew Day

Date: _____

Brewer(s): _____

Time Started: _____

Temperature: _____

☐ Mash/Steep (if using grains)

Grain Crush: ☐ Coarse ☐ Medium ☐ Fine ☐ Flour

Ingredient Notes (Does the malt smell fresh? Firm or mushy?): _____

_____

Strike Water: Amount: _____ Temperature: _____

Mash/Steep Temperature(s): _____

Type of Sparge: ☐ Fly ☐ Batch ☐ No

Sparge Water: Amount: _____ Temperature: _____

First Runnings Gravity: _____

Final Runnings Gravity: _____

Notes: _____

_____

_____

Time Mash/Steep Completed: _____

☐ Boil

Boil Vessel: _____

Heat Source: ☐ Gas Stove ☐ Electric Stove ☐ Propane Burner
              ☐ Electric Heater ☐ Other

Wort Collected: _____

Initial Boil Gravity: (*Stir the boil point vigorously for a minute to ensure even sugar mixing.*) _____

Time to Start Boil: _____

Time at Start of Boil: _____

Extract Added: ☐ Start of boil ☐ Late: _____ minutes

☐ Scum Skimmed

Boil Notes (vigor, etc): _____

_____

Hops (as needed)

☐ _____ Minute Addition   ☐ _____ Minute Addition

☐ _____ Minute Addition   ☐ _____ Minute Addition

☐ _____ Minute Addition   ☐ _____ Minute Addition

☐ _____ Minute Addition

Notes: _____

_____

_____

☐ Adding Other Ingredients

Notes: _____

_____

_____

Time Boil Ended: _____

☐ Whirlpool

How Long?: _____

☐ Chill Wort

Cooling Mechanism: ☐ Closed Pot Overnight   ☐ Sink/Ice Bath

☐ Immersion Coil   ☐ Whirlpool Immersion   ☐ Counterflow Chiller

Chilling Start Time: _____

Water/Bath Temperature: _____

Temperature of Wort when Fully Chilled: _____

Chilling Finish Time: _____

☐ Hydrometer Reading:

Original gravity (O.G.) _____

☐ Notes on pitching the yeast

_____

_____

_____

Temperature of the wort when the yeast is pitched: _____

☐ Used Starter

☐ Decanted Starter

Brew Day Finished: _____

Fermentation

Date: _____

Fermenter Type: ☐ Bucket   ☐ Glass Carboy   ☐ Plastic Carboy

               ☐ Keg   ☐ Conical   ☐ Other: _____

Fermenter Closure: ☐ Airlock   ☐ Blow-off Tube   ☐ Foil Cap   ☐ Open

Length of Ferment: _____ Days

Aroma and Visual Notes: _____

_____

_____

_____

Ferment Temperature

Try to keep the temperature constant throughout the ferment.

Date: _____ Temp: _____

Date: _____ Temp: _____

Date: _____ Temp: _____

Date: _____ Temp: _____

Secondary Fermentation (if applicable)

Date: _____

Gravity at Transfer: _____

Length of Ferment: _____ Days

Aroma and Visual Notes: _____

_____

_____

_____

Additions to Secondary: _____

_____

_____

Finings/Clarification Aids: _____

_____

_____

Packaging

Date: _____

Hydrometer Reading: _____
(This number is the Final Gravity, or FG).

Calculate Alcohol by Volume (or ABV):

$$\underset{\text{Alcohol By Volume}}{\underline{\hspace{3cm}}} = (\underset{\text{Original Gravity}}{\underline{\hspace{3cm}}} - \underset{\text{Final Gravity}}{\underline{\hspace{3cm}}}) / 7.5$$

Calculating Attenuation

$$\underset{\text{Apparent Attenuation}}{\underline{\hspace{3cm}}} = 100 \times ((\underset{\text{Original Gravity}}{\underline{\hspace{3cm}}} - \underset{\text{Final Gravity}}{\underline{\hspace{3cm}}}) / \underset{\text{Original Gravity}}{\underline{\hspace{3cm}}})$$

PACKAGE

☐ Bottle   ☐ Keg

CARBONATION

Desired Level of Carbonation: _____

☐ Primed

    with (sugar, wort, etc): _____

How much: _____

☐ Forced

Beer Temp: _____

CO_2 Setting: _____ p.s.i.

Method: ☐ Steady Pressure _____ week(s)

       ☐ Fast Carbonation: Shake at _____ p.s.i. for _____ minutes

Beer Storage Temperature: _____

The Final Beer

Chill and test a bottle. If carbonated, you're ready! Otherwise, wait another week and repeat. As you take notes, record how the beer changes as it warms up and lets off more CO_2.

Beer Temperature: _____

Pour Notes (carbonation, head, cloudy, etc.): _____

_____

Aroma Notes (What do you smell from the hops, the malt and the yeast?) _____

_____

_____

Appearance Notes (clarity, color, etc.)

_____

_____

Taste Notes (What tastes do you perceive from the ingredients?)

_____

_____

Mouth Feel/Finish

_____

_____

Overall Notes

_____

_____

_____

Circle all that apply

Bitter Buttery Cooked Sweet Hoppy Fruity Harsh Malty Metallic

Spicy Roasted Smoky Watery Yeasty Acidic Sour Clean Earthy

Impressions that Change with Temperature/Time: _____

_____

What Worked? _____

_____

What Didn't Work? _____

_____

What Changes Do I Want to Make? _____

_____

_____

Overall Score (0–50) _____

Competition Notes (If you enter the beer in a competition, record the judges' impressions and scores.)

Competition Name: _____

Date: _____ Score: _____ Award: _____

Judge Notes: _____

_____

_____

_____

Competition Name: _____

Date: _____ Score: _____ Award: _____

Judge Notes: _____

_____

_____

_____

Competition Name: _____

Date: _____ Score: _____ Award: _____

Judge Notes: _____

_____

_____

_____

Competition Name: _____

Date: _____ Score: _____ Award: _____

Judge Notes: _____

_____

_____

_____

The Beer

Style: _____

Brew Type: ☐ Extract   ☐ Extract with Steeped Grains
                  ☐ Partial Mash   ☐ All Grain

The Beer Story: _____
_____
_____
_____
_____

Desired Flavor and Aromas: _____
_____
_____

Gallons: _____   SRM (Color): _____

OG: _____   IBUs: _____

ABV: _____   Boil Time: _____

Ingredients

Malt/Grains/Sugar (if used)		
Amount	**Ingredient**	**Brand**

Extract (if used)		
Amount	Ingredient	Brand

Hops				
Amount	Variety	Type	AA %	Time in Boil

Type of Water: _____

Water: ☐ Bottled   ☐ Distilled/R.O.   ☐ Filtered

Water Salts: _____

Other Ingredients		
Amount	Ingredient	Add When?

The Recipe

Yeast: _____

_____

Starter Size: _____ Starter Gravity: _____ Days Fermented: _____

☐ Cold Crashed

Procedures

Mash Type: ☐ Steep   ☐ Single Infusion Mash
              ☐ Step Infusion Mash   ☐ Decoction

Mash Schedule			
Step	Target Temp	Rest Time	Infusion/Direct

Packaging

Dry Hop Schedule (if Dry Hopping)			
Amount	Variety	Temp	Days

Flavor Additions (e.g. vanilla, oak)	
Amount	Ingredient

Preparation

☐ Purchased all ingredients

☐ Equipment all accounted for

Total Cost: $ _____

Inventory Notes

_____

_____

_____

_____

_____

_____

_____

_____

Recipe Thoughts

Why choose the ingredients/techniques specified?

_____

_____

_____

_____

_____

_____

_____

_____

_____

_____

_____

_____

_____

Brew Day

Date: _____

Brewer(s): _____

Time Started: _____

Temperature: _____

☐ Mash/Steep (if using grains)

Grain Crush: ☐ Coarse   ☐ Medium   ☐ Fine   ☐ Flour

Ingredient Notes (Does the malt smell fresh? Firm or mushy?): _____

_____

Strike Water: Amount: _____   Temperature: _____

Mash/Steep Temperature(s): _____

Type of Sparge: ☐ Fly   ☐ Batch   ☐ No

Sparge Water: Amount: _____   Temperature: _____

First Runnings Gravity: _____

Final Runnings Gravity: _____

Notes: _____

_____

_____

Time Mash/Steep Completed: _____

☐ Boil

Boil Vessel: _____

Heat Source: ☐ Gas Stove   ☐ Electric Stove   ☐ Propane Burner

                ☐ Electric Heater   ☐ Other

Wort Collected: _____

Initial Boil Gravity: (*Stir the boil point vigorously for a minute to ensure even*

sugar mixing.) _____

Time to Start Boil: _____

Time at Start of Boil: _____

Extract Added: ☐ Start of boil   ☐ Late: _____ minutes

☐ Scum Skimmed

Boil Notes (vigor, etc): _____

_____

Hops (as needed)

☐ _____ Minute Addition   ☐ _____ Minute Addition

☐ _____ Minute Addition   ☐ _____ Minute Addition

☐ _____ Minute Addition   ☐ _____ Minute Addition

☐ _____ Minute Addition

Notes: _____

_____

_____

☐ Adding Other Ingredients

Notes: _____

_____

_____

Time Boil Ended: _____

☐ Whirlpool

How Long?: _____

☐ Chill Wort

Cooling Mechanism: ☐ Closed Pot Overnight   ☐ Sink/Ice Bath

☐ Immersion Coil   ☐ Whirlpool Immersion   ☐ Counterflow Chiller

Chilling Start Time: _____

Water/Bath Temperature: _____

Temperature of Wort when Fully Chilled: _____

Chilling Finish Time: _____

☐ Hydrometer Reading:

    Original gravity (O.G.) _____

☐ Notes on pitching the yeast

_____

_____

_____

Temperature of the wort when the yeast is pitched: _____

☐ Used Starter

☐ Decanted Starter

Brew Day Finished: _____

Fermentation

Date: _____

Fermenter Type: ☐ Bucket ☐ Glass Carboy ☐ Plastic Carboy

☐ Keg ☐ Conical ☐ Other: _____

Fermenter Closure: ☐ Airlock ☐ Blow-off Tube ☐ Foil Cap ☐ Open

Length of Ferment: _____ Days

Aroma and Visual Notes: _____

_____

_____

_____

Ferment Temperature

Try to keep the temperature constant throughout the ferment.

Date: _____ Temp: _____

Date: _____ Temp: _____

Date: _____ Temp: _____

Date: _____ Temp: _____

Secondary Fermentation (if applicable)

Date: _____

Gravity at Transfer: _____

Length of Ferment: _____ Days

Aroma and Visual Notes: _____

_____

_____

_____

Additions to Secondary: _____

_____

_____

Finings/Clarification Aids: _____

_____

_____

Packaging

Date: _____

Hydrometer Reading: _____
(This number is the Final Gravity, or FG).

Calculate Alcohol by Volume (or ABV):

$$\underline{\hspace{3cm}} = (\underline{\hspace{3cm}} - \underline{\hspace{3cm}}) / 7.5$$
Alcohol By Volume = (Original Gravity − Final Gravity) / 7.5

Calculating Attenuation

$$\underline{\hspace{3cm}} = 100 \times ((\underline{\hspace{3cm}} - \underline{\hspace{3cm}}) / \underline{\hspace{3cm}})$$
Apparent Attenuation = 100 × ((Original Gravity − Final Gravity) / Original Gravity)

PACKAGE

☐ Bottle   ☐ Keg

CARBONATION

Desired Level of Carbonation: _____

☐ Primed

    with (sugar, wort, etc): _____

How much: _____

☐ Forced

Beer Temp: _____

CO_2 Setting: _____ p.s.i.

Method: ☐ Steady Pressure _____ week(s)

    ☐ Fast Carbonation: Shake at _____ p.s.i. for _____ minutes

Beer Storage Temperature: _____

The Final Beer

Chill and test a bottle. If carbonated, you're ready! Otherwise, wait another week and repeat. As you take notes, record how the beer changes as it warms up and lets off more CO_2.

Beer Temperature: _____

Pour Notes (carbonation, head, cloudy, etc.): _____

Aroma Notes (What do you smell from the hops, the malt and the yeast?) _____

Appearance Notes (clarity, color, etc.)

Taste Notes (What tastes do you perceive from the ingredients?)

Mouth Feel/Finish

Overall Notes

Circle all that apply

Bitter   Buttery   Cooked   Sweet   Hoppy   Fruity   Harsh   Malty   Metallic
Spicy   Roasted   Smoky   Watery   Yeasty   Acidic   Sour   Clean   Earthy

Impressions that Change with Temperature/Time: _____

What Worked? _____

What Didn't Work? _____

_____

What Changes Do I Want to Make? _____

_____

_____

Overall Score (0–50) _____

Competition Notes (If you enter the beer in a competition, record the judges' impressions and scores.)

Competition Name: _____

Date: _____ Score: _____ Award: _____

Judge Notes: _____

_____

_____

_____

Competition Name: _____

Date: _____ Score: _____ Award: _____

Judge Notes: _____

_____

_____

_____

Competition Name: _____

Date: _____ Score: _____ Award: _____

Judge Notes: _____

_____

_____

_____

Competition Name: _____

Date: _____ Score: _____ Award: _____

Judge Notes: _____

_____

_____

_____

The Beer

Style: _____

Brew Type: ☐ Extract   ☐ Extract with Steeped Grains
            ☐ Partial Mash   ☐ All Grain

The Beer Story: _____

_____

_____

_____

_____

Desired Flavor and Aromas: _____

_____

_____

Gallons: _____   SRM (Color): _____

OG: _____   IBUs: _____

ABV: _____   Boil Time: _____

Ingredients

Malt/Grains/Sugar (if used)		
Amount	Ingredient	Brand

Extract (if used)		
Amount	Ingredient	Brand

Hops				
Amount	Variety	Type	AA %	Time in Boil

Type of Water: _____

Water: ☐ Bottled   ☐ Distilled/R.O.   ☐ Filtered

Water Salts: _____

Other Ingredients		
Amount	Ingredient	Add When?

The Recipe

Yeast: _____

_____

Starter Size: _____ Starter Gravity: _____ Days Fermented: _____

☐ Cold Crashed

Procedures

Mash Type: ☐ Steep   ☐ Single Infusion Mash
          ☐ Step Infusion Mash   ☐ Decoction

Mash Schedule			
Step	Target Temp	Rest Time	Infusion/Direct

Packaging

Dry Hop Schedule (if Dry Hopping)			
Amount	Variety	Temp	Days

Flavor Additions (e.g. vanilla, oak)	
Amount	Ingredient

Preparation

☐ Purchased all ingredients

☐ Equipment all accounted for

Total Cost: $ _____

Inventory Notes

_____
_____
_____
_____
_____
_____
_____
_____

Recipe Thoughts

Why choose the ingredients/techniques specified?

_____
_____
_____
_____
_____
_____
_____
_____
_____
_____
_____
_____
_____
_____
_____

Brew Day

Date: _____

Brewer(s): _____

Time Started: _____

Temperature: _____

☐ Mash/Steep (if using grains)

Grain Crush: ☐ Coarse   ☐ Medium   ☐ Fine   ☐ Flour

Ingredient Notes (Does the malt smell fresh? Firm or mushy?): _____

_____

Strike Water: Amount: _____   Temperature: _____

Mash/Steep Temperature(s): _____

Type of Sparge: ☐ Fly   ☐ Batch   ☐ No

Sparge Water: Amount: _____   Temperature: _____

First Runnings Gravity: _____

Final Runnings Gravity: _____

Notes: _____

_____

_____

Time Mash/Steep Completed: _____

☐ Boil

Boil Vessel: _____

Heat Source: ☐ Gas Stove   ☐ Electric Stove   ☐ Propane Burner

                ☐ Electric Heater   ☐ Other

Wort Collected: _____

Initial Boil Gravity: (*Stir the boil point vigorously for a minute to ensure even*

sugar mixing.) _____

Time to Start Boil: _____

Time at Start of Boil: _____

Extract Added: ☐ Start of boil   ☐ Late: _____ minutes

☐ Scum Skimmed

Boil Notes (vigor, etc): _____

_____

Hops (as needed)

☐ _____ Minute Addition   ☐ _____ Minute Addition

☐ _____ Minute Addition   ☐ _____ Minute Addition

☐ _____ Minute Addition   ☐ _____ Minute Addition

☐ _____ Minute Addition

Notes: _____

_____

_____

☐ Adding Other Ingredients

Notes: _____

_____

_____

Time Boil Ended: _____

☐ Whirlpool

How Long?: _____

☐ Chill Wort

Cooling Mechanism: ☐ Closed Pot Overnight   ☐ Sink/Ice Bath

☐ Immersion Coil   ☐ Whirlpool Immersion   ☐ Counterflow Chiller

Chilling Start Time: _____

Water/Bath Temperature: _____

Temperature of Wort when Fully Chilled: _____

Chilling Finish Time: _____

☐ Hydrometer Reading:

    Original gravity (O.G.) _____

☐ Notes on pitching the yeast

_____

_____

_____

Temperature of the wort when the yeast is pitched: _____

☐ Used Starter

☐ Decanted Starter

Brew Day Finished: _____

Fermentation

Date: _____

Fermenter Type: ☐ Bucket   ☐ Glass Carboy   ☐ Plastic Carboy

☐ Keg   ☐ Conical   ☐ Other: _____

Fermenter Closure: ☐ Airlock   ☐ Blow-off Tube   ☐ Foil Cap   ☐ Open

Length of Ferment: _____ Days

Aroma and Visual Notes: _____

_____

_____

_____

Ferment Temperature

Try to keep the temperature constant throughout the ferment.

Date: _____   Temp: _____

Date: _____   Temp: _____

Date: _____   Temp: _____

Date: _____   Temp: _____

Secondary Fermentation (if applicable)

Date: _____

Gravity at Transfer: _____

Length of Ferment: _____ Days

Aroma and Visual Notes: _____

_____

_____

_____

Additions to Secondary: _____

_____

_____

Finings/Clarification Aids: _____

_____

_____

Packaging

Date: _____

Hydrometer Reading: _____
(This number is the Final Gravity, or FG).

Calculate Alcohol by Volume (or ABV):

$$\underset{\text{Alcohol By Volume}}{\underline{\hspace{3cm}}} = (\underset{\text{Original Gravity}}{\underline{\hspace{3cm}}} - \underset{\text{Final Gravity}}{\underline{\hspace{3cm}}}) / 7.5$$

Calculating Attenuation

$$\underset{\text{Apparent Attenuation}}{\underline{\hspace{3cm}}} = 100 \times ((\underset{\text{Original Gravity}}{\underline{\hspace{3cm}}} - \underset{\text{Final Gravity}}{\underline{\hspace{3cm}}}) / \underset{\text{Original Gravity}}{\underline{\hspace{3cm}}})$$

PACKAGE

☐ Bottle   ☐ Keg

CARBONATION

Desired Level of Carbonation: _____

☐ Primed

　　with (sugar, wort, etc): _____

How much: _____

☐ Forced

Beer Temp: _____

CO_2 Setting: _____ p.s.i.

Method: ☐ Steady Pressure _____ week(s)

　　　　　☐ Fast Carbonation: Shake at _____ p.s.i. for _____ minutes

Beer Storage Temperature: _____

The Final Beer

Chill and test a bottle. If carbonated, you're ready! Otherwise, wait another week and repeat. As you take notes, record how the beer changes as it warms up and lets off more CO_2.

Beer Temperature: _____

Pour Notes (carbonation, head, cloudy, etc.): _____

_____

Aroma Notes (What do you smell from the hops, the malt and the yeast?) _____

_____

_____

Appearance Notes (clarity, color, etc.)

_____

_____

Taste Notes (What tastes do you perceive from the ingredients?)

_____

_____

Mouth Feel/Finish

_____

_____

Overall Notes

_____

_____

_____

Circle all that apply

Bitter   Buttery   Cooked   Sweet   Hoppy   Fruity   Harsh   Malty   Metallic

Spicy   Roasted   Smoky   Watery   Yeasty   Acidic   Sour   Clean   Earthy

Impressions that Change with Temperature/Time: _____

_____

What Worked? _____

_____

What Didn't Work? _____

_____

What Changes Do I Want to Make? _____

_____

_____

Overall Score (0–50) _____

Competition Notes (If you enter the beer in a competition, record the judges' impressions and scores.)

Competition Name: _____

Date: _____ Score: _____ Award: _____

Judge Notes: _____

_____

_____

_____

Competition Name: _____

Date: _____ Score: _____ Award: _____

Judge Notes: _____

_____

_____

_____

Competition Name: _____

Date: _____ Score: _____ Award: _____

Judge Notes: _____

_____

_____

_____

Competition Name: _____

Date: _____ Score: _____ Award: _____

Judge Notes: _____

_____

_____

_____

The Beer

Style: _____

Brew Type: ☐ Extract ☐ Extract with Steeped Grains
☐ Partial Mash ☐ All Grain

The Beer Story: _____

_____

_____

_____

_____

Desired Flavor and Aromas: _____

_____

_____

Gallons: _____ SRM (Color): _____

OG: _____ IBUs: _____

ABV: _____ Boil Time: _____

Ingredients

Malt/Grains/Sugar (if used)		
Amount	Ingredient	Brand

Extract (if used)

Amount	Ingredient	Brand

Hops

Amount	Variety	Type	AA %	Time in Boil

Type of Water: _____

Water: ☐ Bottled   ☐ Distilled/R.O.   ☐ Filtered

Water Salts: _____

Other Ingredients

Amount	Ingredient	Add When?

The Recipe

Yeast: _____

_____

Starter Size: _____ Starter Gravity: _____ Days Fermented: _____

☐ Cold Crashed

Procedures

Mash Type: ☐ Steep   ☐ Single Infusion Mash
           ☐ Step Infusion Mash   ☐ Decoction

Mash Schedule			
Step	Target Temp	Rest Time	Infusion/Direct

Packaging

Dry Hop Schedule (if Dry Hopping)			
Amount	Variety	Temp	Days

Flavor Additions (e.g. vanilla, oak)	
Amount	Ingredient

Preparation

☐ Purchased all ingredients

☐ Equipment all accounted for

Total Cost: $ _____

Inventory Notes

_____
_____
_____
_____
_____
_____
_____
_____

Recipe Thoughts

Why choose the ingredients/techniques specified?

_____
_____
_____
_____
_____
_____
_____
_____
_____
_____
_____
_____

Brew Day

Date: _____

Brewer(s): _____

Time Started: _____

Temperature: _____

☐ **Mash/Steep (if using grains)**

Grain Crush: ☐ Coarse ☐ Medium ☐ Fine ☐ Flour

Ingredient Notes (Does the malt smell fresh? Firm or mushy?): _____

_____

Strike Water: Amount: _____ Temperature: _____

Mash/Steep Temperature(s): _____

Type of Sparge: ☐ Fly ☐ Batch ☐ No

Sparge Water: Amount: _____ Temperature: _____

First Runnings Gravity: _____

Final Runnings Gravity: _____

Notes: _____

_____

_____

Time Mash/Steep Completed: _____

☐ **Boil**

Boil Vessel: _____

Heat Source: ☐ Gas Stove ☐ Electric Stove ☐ Propane Burner
              ☐ Electric Heater ☐ Other

Wort Collected: _____

Initial Boil Gravity: (*Stir the boil point vigorously for a minute to ensure even sugar mixing.*) _____

Time to Start Boil: _____

Time at Start of Boil: _____

Extract Added: ☐ Start of boil ☐ Late: _____ minutes

☐ Scum Skimmed

Boil Notes (vigor, etc): _____

_____

Hops (as needed)

☐ _____ Minute Addition   ☐ _____ Minute Addition

☐ _____ Minute Addition   ☐ _____ Minute Addition

☐ _____ Minute Addition   ☐ _____ Minute Addition

☐ _____ Minute Addition

Notes: _____

_____

_____

☐ Adding Other Ingredients

Notes: _____

_____

_____

Time Boil Ended: _____

☐ Whirlpool

How Long?: _____

☐ Chill Wort

Cooling Mechanism: ☐ Closed Pot Overnight   ☐ Sink/Ice Bath

☐ Immersion Coil   ☐ Whirlpool Immersion   ☐ Counterflow Chiller

Chilling Start Time: _____

Water/Bath Temperature: _____

Temperature of Wort when Fully Chilled: _____

Chilling Finish Time: _____

☐ Hydrometer Reading:

    Original gravity (O.G.) _____

☐ Notes on pitching the yeast

_____

_____

_____

Temperature of the wort when the yeast is pitched: _____

☐ Used Starter

☐ Decanted Starter

Brew Day Finished: _____

Fermentation

Date: _____

Fermenter Type: ☐ Bucket   ☐ Glass Carboy   ☐ Plastic Carboy

                  ☐ Keg   ☐ Conical   ☐ Other: _____

Fermenter Closure: ☐ Airlock   ☐ Blow-off Tube   ☐ Foil Cap   ☐ Open

Length of Ferment: _____ Days

Aroma and Visual Notes: _____

_____

_____

_____

Ferment Temperature

Try to keep the temperature constant throughout the ferment.

Date: _____ Temp: _____

Date: _____ Temp: _____

Date: _____ Temp: _____

Date: _____ Temp: _____

Secondary Fermentation (if applicable)

Date: _____

Gravity at Transfer: _____

Length of Ferment: _____ Days

Aroma and Visual Notes: _____

_____

_____

_____

Additions to Secondary: _____

_____

_____

Finings/Clarification Aids: _____

_____

_____

Packaging

Date: _____

Hydrometer Reading: _____
(This number is the Final Gravity, or FG).

Calculate Alcohol by Volume (or ABV):

$$\underset{\text{Alcohol By Volume}}{\underline{\hspace{3cm}}} = (\underset{\text{Original Gravity}}{\underline{\hspace{3cm}}} - \underset{\text{Final Gravity}}{\underline{\hspace{3cm}}}) / 7.5$$

Calculating Attenuation

$$\underset{\text{Apparent Attenuation}}{\underline{\hspace{2.5cm}}} = 100 \times ((\underset{\text{Original Gravity}}{\underline{\hspace{2.5cm}}} - \underset{\text{Final Gravity}}{\underline{\hspace{2.5cm}}}) / \underset{\text{Original Gravity}}{\underline{\hspace{2.5cm}}})$$

PACKAGE

☐ Bottle   ☐ Keg

CARBONATION

Desired Level of Carbonation: _____

☐ Primed

   with (sugar, wort, etc): _____

How much: _____

☐ Forced

Beer Temp: _____

CO_2 Setting: _____ p.s.i.

Method: ☐ Steady Pressure _____ week(s)

       ☐ Fast Carbonation: Shake at _____ p.s.i. for _____ minutes

Beer Storage Temperature: _____

The Final Beer

Chill and test a bottle. If carbonated, you're ready! Otherwise, wait another week and repeat. As you take notes, record how the beer changes as it warms up and lets off more CO_2.

Beer Temperature: _____

Pour Notes (carbonation, head, cloudy, etc.): _____

Aroma Notes (What do you smell from the hops, the malt and the yeast?) _____

_____

Appearance Notes (clarity, color, etc.)

_____

Taste Notes (What tastes do you perceive from the ingredients?)

_____

Mouth Feel/Finish

_____

Overall Notes

_____

_____

Circle all that apply

Bitter Buttery Cooked Sweet Hoppy Fruity Harsh Malty Metallic
Spicy Roasted Smoky Watery Yeasty Acidic Sour Clean Earthy

Impressions that Change with Temperature/Time: _____

_____

What Worked? _____

_____

What Didn't Work? _____

_____

What Changes Do I Want to Make? _____

_____

_____

Overall Score (0–50) _____

Competition Notes (If you enter the beer in a competition, record the judges' impressions and scores.)

Competition Name: _____

Date: _____ Score: _____ Award: _____

Judge Notes: _____

_____

_____

_____

Competition Name: _____

Date: _____ Score: _____ Award: _____

Judge Notes: _____

_____

_____

_____

Competition Name: _____

Date: _____ Score: _____ Award: _____

Judge Notes: _____

_____

_____

_____

Competition Name: _____

Date: _____ Score: _____ Award: _____

Judge Notes: _____

_____

_____

_____

The Beer

Style: _____

Brew Type: ☐ Extract   ☐ Extract with Steeped Grains
            ☐ Partial Mash   ☐ All Grain

The Beer Story: _____
_____
_____
_____
_____

Desired Flavor and Aromas: _____
_____
_____

Gallons: _____   SRM (Color): _____
OG: _____   IBUs: _____
ABV: _____   Boil Time: _____

Ingredients

Malt/Grains/Sugar (if used)		
Amount	Ingredient	Brand

Extract (if used)		
Amount	Ingredient	Brand

Hops				
Amount	Variety	Type	AA %	Time in Boil

Type of Water: _____

Water: ☐ Bottled   ☐ Distilled/R.O.   ☐ Filtered

Water Salts: _____

Other Ingredients		
Amount	Ingredient	Add When?

The Recipe

Yeast: _____

_____

Starter Size: _____ Starter Gravity: _____ Days Fermented: _____

☐ Cold Crashed

Procedures

Mash Type: ☐ Steep   ☐ Single Infusion Mash
             ☐ Step Infusion Mash   ☐ Decoction

Mash Schedule			
Step	Target Temp	Rest Time	Infusion/Direct

Packaging

Dry Hop Schedule (if Dry Hopping)			
Amount	Variety	Temp	Days

Flavor Additions (e.g. vanilla, oak)	
Amount	Ingredient

Preparation

☐ Purchased all ingredients

☐ Equipment all accounted for

Total Cost: $ _____

Inventory Notes

_____

_____

_____

_____

_____

_____

_____

_____

Recipe Thoughts

Why choose the ingredients/techniques specified?

_____

_____

_____

_____

_____

_____

_____

_____

_____

_____

_____

_____

_____

Brew Day

Date: _____

Brewer(s): _____

Time Started: _____

Temperature: _____

☐ Mash/Steep (if using grains)

Grain Crush: ☐ Coarse ☐ Medium ☐ Fine ☐ Flour

Ingredient Notes (Does the malt smell fresh? Firm or mushy?): _____

_____

Strike Water: Amount: _____ Temperature: _____

Mash/Steep Temperature(s): _____

Type of Sparge: ☐ Fly ☐ Batch ☐ No

Sparge Water: Amount: _____ Temperature: _____

First Runnings Gravity: _____

Final Runnings Gravity: _____

Notes: _____

_____

_____

Time Mash/Steep Completed: _____

☐ Boil

Boil Vessel: _____

Heat Source: ☐ Gas Stove ☐ Electric Stove ☐ Propane Burner
 ☐ Electric Heater ☐ Other

Wort Collected: _____

Initial Boil Gravity: (*Stir the boil point vigorously for a minute to ensure even sugar mixing.*) _____

Time to Start Boil: _____

Time at Start of Boil: _____

Extract Added: ☐ Start of boil ☐ Late: _____ minutes

☐ Scum Skimmed

Boil Notes (vigor, etc): _____

_____

Hops (as needed)

☐ _____ Minute Addition   ☐ _____ Minute Addition

☐ _____ Minute Addition   ☐ _____ Minute Addition

☐ _____ Minute Addition   ☐ _____ Minute Addition

☐ _____ Minute Addition

Notes: _____

_____

_____

☐ Adding Other Ingredients

Notes: _____

_____

_____

Time Boil Ended: _____

☐ Whirlpool

How Long?: _____

☐ Chill Wort

Cooling Mechanism: ☐ Closed Pot Overnight   ☐ Sink/Ice Bath

☐ Immersion Coil   ☐ Whirlpool Immersion   ☐ Counterflow Chiller

Chilling Start Time: _____

Water/Bath Temperature: _____

Temperature of Wort when Fully Chilled: _____

Chilling Finish Time: _____

☐ Hydrometer Reading:

    Original gravity (O.G.) _____

☐ Notes on pitching the yeast

_____

_____

_____

Temperature of the wort when the yeast is pitched: _____

☐ Used Starter

☐ Decanted Starter

Brew Day Finished: _____

Fermentation

Date: _____

Fermenter Type: ☐ Bucket   ☐ Glass Carboy   ☐ Plastic Carboy
                 ☐ Keg   ☐ Conical   ☐ Other: _____
Fermenter Closure: ☐ Airlock   ☐ Blow-off Tube   ☐ Foil Cap   ☐ Open
Length of Ferment: _____ Days
Aroma and Visual Notes: _____
_____
_____
_____

Ferment Temperature

Try to keep the temperature constant throughout the ferment.

Date: _____ Temp: _____
Date: _____ Temp: _____
Date: _____ Temp: _____
Date: _____ Temp: _____

Secondary Fermentation (if applicable)

Date: _____

Gravity at Transfer: _____
Length of Ferment: _____ Days
Aroma and Visual Notes: _____
_____
_____
_____

Additions to Secondary: _____
_____
_____

Finings/Clarification Aids: _____
_____
_____

Packaging

Date: _____

Hydrometer Reading: _____
(This number is the Final Gravity, or FG).

Calculate Alcohol by Volume (or ABV):

$$\underset{\text{Alcohol By Volume}}{\underline{\hspace{3cm}}} = (\underset{\text{Original Gravity}}{\underline{\hspace{3cm}}} - \underset{\text{Final Gravity}}{\underline{\hspace{3cm}}}) / 7.5$$

Calculating Attenuation

$$\underset{\text{Apparent Attenuation}}{\underline{\hspace{3cm}}} = 100 \times ((\underset{\text{Original Gravity}}{\underline{\hspace{3cm}}} - \underset{\text{Final Gravity}}{\underline{\hspace{3cm}}}) / \underset{\text{Original Gravity}}{\underline{\hspace{3cm}}})$$

PACKAGE

☐ Bottle　☐ Keg

CARBONATION

Desired Level of Carbonation: _____

☐ Primed

　with (sugar, wort, etc): _____

How much: _____

☐ Forced

Beer Temp: _____

CO_2 Setting: _____ p.s.i.

Method:　☐ Steady Pressure _____ week(s)

　　　　☐ Fast Carbonation: Shake at _____ p.s.i. for _____ minutes

Beer Storage Temperature: _____

The Final Beer

Chill and test a bottle. If carbonated, you're ready! Otherwise, wait another week and repeat. As you take notes, record how the beer changes as it warms up and lets off more CO_2.

Beer Temperature: _____

Pour Notes (carbonation, head, cloudy, etc.): _____

_____

Aroma Notes (What do you smell from the hops, the malt and the yeast?) _____

_____

_____

Appearance Notes (clarity, color, etc.)

_____

_____

Taste Notes (What tastes do you perceive from the ingredients?)

_____

_____

Mouth Feel/Finish

_____

_____

Overall Notes

_____

_____

_____

Circle all that apply

Bitter   Buttery   Cooked   Sweet   Hoppy   Fruity   Harsh   Malty   Metallic

Spicy   Roasted   Smoky   Watery   Yeasty   Acidic   Sour   Clean   Earthy

Impressions that Change with Temperature/Time: _____

_____

What Worked? _____

_____

What Didn't Work? _____

_____

What Changes Do I Want to Make? _____

_____

_____

Overall Score (0–50) _____

Competition Notes (If you enter the beer in a competition, record the judges' impressions and scores.)

Competition Name: _____

Date: _____ Score: _____ Award: _____

Judge Notes: _____

_____

_____

_____

Competition Name: _____

Date: _____ Score: _____ Award: _____

Judge Notes: _____

_____

_____

_____

Competition Name: _____

Date: _____ Score: _____ Award: _____

Judge Notes: _____

_____

_____

_____

Competition Name: _____

Date: _____ Score: _____ Award: _____

Judge Notes: _____

_____

_____

_____

The Beer

Style: _____

Brew Type: ☐ Extract   ☐ Extract with Steeped Grains
            ☐ Partial Mash   ☐ All Grain

The Beer Story: _____
_____
_____
_____
_____

Desired Flavor and Aromas: _____
_____
_____

Gallons: _____   SRM (Color): _____
OG: _____   IBUs: _____
ABV: _____   Boil Time: _____

Ingredients

Malt/Grains/Sugar (if used)		
Amount	Ingredient	Brand

Extract (if used)		
Amount	Ingredient	Brand

Hops				
Amount	Variety	Type	AA %	Time in Boil

Type of Water: _____

Water: ☐ Bottled   ☐ Distilled/R.O.   ☐ Filtered

Water Salts: _____

Other Ingredients		
Amount	Ingredient	Add When?

The Recipe

Yeast: _____

_____

Starter Size: _____ Starter Gravity: _____ Days Fermented: _____

☐ Cold Crashed

Procedures

Mash Type: ☐ Steep   ☐ Single Infusion Mash
          ☐ Step Infusion Mash   ☐ Decoction

Mash Schedule			
Step	Target Temp	Rest Time	Infusion/Direct

Packaging

Dry Hop Schedule (if Dry Hopping)			
Amount	Variety	Temp	Days

Flavor Additions (e.g. vanilla, oak)	
Amount	Ingredient

Preparation

☐ Purchased all ingredients

☐ Equipment all accounted for

Total Cost: $ _____

Inventory Notes

_____

_____

_____

_____

_____

_____

_____

_____

Recipe Thoughts

Why choose the ingredients/techniques specified?

_____

_____

_____

_____

_____

_____

_____

_____

_____

_____

_____

_____

_____

Brew Day

Date: _____

Brewer(s): _____

Time Started: _____

Temperature: _____

☐ Mash/Steep (if using grains)

Grain Crush: ☐ Coarse ☐ Medium ☐ Fine ☐ Flour

Ingredient Notes (Does the malt smell fresh? Firm or mushy?): _____

_____

Strike Water: Amount: _____ Temperature: _____

Mash/Steep Temperature(s): _____

Type of Sparge: ☐ Fly ☐ Batch ☐ No

Sparge Water: Amount: _____ Temperature: _____

First Runnings Gravity: _____

Final Runnings Gravity: _____

Notes: _____

_____

_____

Time Mash/Steep Completed: _____

☐ Boil

Boil Vessel: _____

Heat Source: ☐ Gas Stove   ☐ Electric Stove   ☐ Propane Burner

☐ Electric Heater   ☐ Other

Wort Collected: _____

Initial Boil Gravity: (*Stir the boil point vigorously for a minute to ensure even sugar mixing.*) _____

Time to Start Boil: _____

Time at Start of Boil: _____

Extract Added: ☐ Start of boil   ☐ Late: _____ minutes

☐ Scum Skimmed

Boil Notes (vigor, etc): _____

Hops (as needed)

☐ _____ Minute Addition   ☐ _____ Minute Addition

☐ _____ Minute Addition   ☐ _____ Minute Addition

☐ _____ Minute Addition   ☐ _____ Minute Addition

☐ _____ Minute Addition

Notes: _____

_____

_____

☐ Adding Other Ingredients

Notes: _____

_____

_____

Time Boil Ended: _____

☐ Whirlpool

How Long?: _____

☐ Chill Wort

Cooling Mechanism: ☐ Closed Pot Overnight   ☐ Sink/Ice Bath

☐ Immersion Coil   ☐ Whirlpool Immersion   ☐ Counterflow Chiller

Chilling Start Time: _____

Water/Bath Temperature: _____

Temperature of Wort when Fully Chilled: _____

Chilling Finish Time: _____

☐ Hydrometer Reading:

   Original gravity (O.G.) _____

☐ Notes on pitching the yeast

_____

_____

_____

Temperature of the wort when the yeast is pitched: _____

☐ Used Starter

☐ Decanted Starter

Brew Day Finished: _____

Fermentation

Date: _____

Fermenter Type: ☐ Bucket   ☐ Glass Carboy   ☐ Plastic Carboy
                ☐ Keg   ☐ Conical   ☐ Other: _____

Fermenter Closure: ☐ Airlock   ☐ Blow-off Tube   ☐ Foil Cap   ☐ Open

Length of Ferment: _____ Days

Aroma and Visual Notes: _____

_____

_____

_____

Ferment Temperature

Try to keep the temperature constant throughout the ferment.

Date: _____   Temp: _____

Date: _____   Temp: _____

Date: _____   Temp: _____

Date: _____   Temp: _____

Secondary Fermentation (if applicable)

Date: _____

Gravity at Transfer: _____

Length of Ferment: _____ Days

Aroma and Visual Notes: _____

_____

_____

_____

Additions to Secondary: _____

_____

_____

Finings/Clarification Aids: _____

_____

_____

Packaging

Date: _____

Hydrometer Reading: _____
(This number is the Final Gravity, or FG).

Calculate Alcohol by Volume (or ABV):

$$\underset{\text{Alcohol By Volume}}{\underline{\hspace{3cm}}} = (\underset{\text{Original Gravity}}{\underline{\hspace{3cm}}} - \underset{\text{Final Gravity}}{\underline{\hspace{3cm}}}) / 7.5$$

Calculating Attenuation

$$\underset{\text{Apparent Attenuation}}{\underline{\hspace{3cm}}} = 100 \times ((\underset{\text{Original Gravity}}{\underline{\hspace{3cm}}} - \underset{\text{Final Gravity}}{\underline{\hspace{3cm}}}) / \underset{\text{Original Gravity}}{\underline{\hspace{3cm}}})$$

PACKAGE

☐ Bottle   ☐ Keg

CARBONATION

Desired Level of Carbonation: _____

☐ Primed

    with (sugar, wort, etc): _____

How much: _____

☐ Forced

Beer Temp: _____

CO_2 Setting: _____ p.s.i.

Method: ☐ Steady Pressure _____ week(s)

      ☐ Fast Carbonation: Shake at _____ p.s.i. for _____ minutes

Beer Storage Temperature: _____

The Final Beer

Chill and test a bottle. If carbonated, you're ready! Otherwise, wait another week and repeat. As you take notes, record how the beer changes as it warms up and lets off more CO_2.

Beer Temperature: _____

Pour Notes (carbonation, head, cloudy, etc.): _____

_____

Aroma Notes (What do you smell from the hops, the malt and the yeast?) _____

_____

_____

Appearance Notes (clarity, color, etc.)

_____

_____

Taste Notes (What tastes do you perceive from the ingredients?)

_____

_____

Mouth Feel/Finish

_____

_____

Overall Notes

_____

_____

_____

Circle all that apply

Bitter   Buttery   Cooked   Sweet   Hoppy   Fruity   Harsh   Malty   Metallic

Spicy   Roasted   Smoky   Watery   Yeasty   Acidic   Sour   Clean   Earthy

Impressions that Change with Temperature/Time: _____

_____

What Worked? _____

_____

What Didn't Work? _____

_____

What Changes Do I Want to Make? _____

_____

_____

Overall Score (0–50) _____

Competition Notes (If you enter the beer in a competition, record the judges' impressions and scores.)

Competition Name: _____

Date: _____ Score: _____ Award: _____

Judge Notes: _____

_____

_____

_____

Competition Name: _____

Date: _____ Score: _____ Award: _____

Judge Notes: _____

_____

_____

_____

Competition Name: _____

Date: _____ Score: _____ Award: _____

Judge Notes: _____

_____

_____

_____

Competition Name: _____

Date: _____ Score: _____ Award: _____

Judge Notes: _____

_____

_____

_____

The Beer

Style: _____

Brew Type: ☐ Extract   ☐ Extract with Steeped Grains
            ☐ Partial Mash   ☐ All Grain

The Beer Story: _____

_____

_____

_____

_____

Desired Flavor and Aromas: _____

_____

_____

Gallons: _____   SRM (Color): _____

OG: _____   IBUs: _____

ABV: _____   Boil Time: _____

Ingredients

Malt / Grains / Sugar (if used)		
Amount	Ingredient	Brand

Extract (if used)

Amount	Ingredient	Brand

Hops

Amount	Variety	Type	AA %	Time in Boil

Type of Water: _____

Water: ☐ Bottled   ☐ Distilled/R.O.   ☐ Filtered

Water Salts: _____

Other Ingredients

Amount	Ingredient	Add When?

The Recipe

Yeast: _____

_____

Starter Size: _____ Starter Gravity: _____ Days Fermented: _____

☐ Cold Crashed

Procedures

Mash Type: ☐ Steep   ☐ Single Infusion Mash
          ☐ Step Infusion Mash   ☐ Decoction

Mash Schedule			
Step	Target Temp	Rest Time	Infusion/Direct

Packaging

Dry Hop Schedule (if Dry Hopping)			
Amount	Variety	Temp	Days

Flavor Additions (e.g. vanilla, oak)	
Amount	Ingredient

Preparation

☐ Purchased all ingredients

☐ Equipment all accounted for

Total Cost: $ _____

Inventory Notes

_____

_____

_____

_____

_____

_____

_____

_____

Recipe Thoughts

Why choose the ingredients/techniques specified?

_____

_____

_____

_____

_____

_____

_____

_____

_____

_____

_____

_____

_____

_____

Brew Day

Date: _____

Brewer(s): _____

Time Started: _____

Temperature: _____

☐ Mash/Steep (if using grains)

Grain Crush: ☐ Coarse   ☐ Medium   ☐ Fine   ☐ Flour

Ingredient Notes (Does the malt smell fresh? Firm or mushy?): _____

_____

Strike Water: Amount: _____   Temperature: _____

Mash/Steep Temperature(s): _____

Type of Sparge: ☐ Fly   ☐ Batch   ☐ No

Sparge Water: Amount: _____   Temperature: _____

First Runnings Gravity: _____

Final Runnings Gravity: _____

Notes: _____

_____

_____

Time Mash/Steep Completed: _____

☐ Boil

Boil Vessel: _____

Heat Source: ☐ Gas Stove   ☐ Electric Stove   ☐ Propane Burner

☐ Electric Heater   ☐ Other

Wort Collected: _____

Initial Boil Gravity: (*Stir the boil point vigorously for a minute to ensure even sugar mixing.*) _____

Time to Start Boil: _____

Time at Start of Boil: _____

Extract Added: ☐ Start of boil   ☐ Late: _____ minutes

☐ Scum Skimmed

Boil Notes (vigor, etc): _____

_____

Hops (as needed)

☐ _____ Minute Addition   ☐ _____ Minute Addition

☐ _____ Minute Addition   ☐ _____ Minute Addition

☐ _____ Minute Addition   ☐ _____ Minute Addition

☐ _____ Minute Addition

Notes: _____

_____

_____

☐ Adding Other Ingredients

Notes: _____

_____

_____

Time Boil Ended: _____

☐ Whirlpool

How Long?: _____

☐ Chill Wort

Cooling Mechanism: ☐ Closed Pot Overnight   ☐ Sink/Ice Bath

☐ Immersion Coil   ☐ Whirlpool Immersion   ☐ Counterflow Chiller

Chilling Start Time: _____

Water/Bath Temperature: _____

Temperature of Wort when Fully Chilled: _____

Chilling Finish Time: _____

☐ Hydrometer Reading:

Original gravity (O.G.) _____

☐ Notes on pitching the yeast

_____

_____

_____

Temperature of the wort when the yeast is pitched: _____

☐ Used Starter

☐ Decanted Starter

Brew Day Finished: _____

Fermentation

Date: _____

Fermenter Type: ☐ Bucket ☐ Glass Carboy ☐ Plastic Carboy
                 ☐ Keg   ☐ Conical   ☐ Other: _____

Fermenter Closure: ☐ Airlock ☐ Blow-off Tube ☐ Foil Cap ☐ Open

Length of Ferment: _____ Days

Aroma and Visual Notes: _____

_____

_____

_____

Ferment Temperature

Try to keep the temperature constant throughout the ferment.

Date: _____ Temp: _____

Date: _____ Temp: _____

Date: _____ Temp: _____

Date: _____ Temp: _____

Secondary Fermentation (if applicable)

Date: _____

Gravity at Transfer: _____

Length of Ferment: _____ Days

Aroma and Visual Notes: _____

_____

_____

_____

Additions to Secondary: _____

_____

_____

Finings/Clarification Aids: _____

_____

_____

Packaging

Date: _____

Hydrometer Reading: _____
(This number is the Final Gravity, or FG).

Calculate Alcohol by Volume (or ABV):

$$\underset{\text{Alcohol By Volume}}{\underline{\hspace{2cm}}} = (\underset{\text{Original Gravity}}{\underline{\hspace{2cm}}} - \underset{\text{Final Gravity}}{\underline{\hspace{2cm}}}) / 7.5$$

Calculating Attenuation

$$\underset{\text{Apparent Attenuation}}{\underline{\hspace{2cm}}} = 100 \times ((\underset{\text{Original Gravity}}{\underline{\hspace{2cm}}} - \underset{\text{Final Gravity}}{\underline{\hspace{2cm}}}) / \underset{\text{Original Gravity}}{\underline{\hspace{2cm}}})$$

PACKAGE

☐ Bottle   ☐ Keg

CARBONATION

Desired Level of Carbonation: _____

☐ Primed

   with (sugar, wort, etc): _____

How much: _____

☐ Forced

Beer Temp: _____

CO_2 Setting: _____ p.s.i.

Method: ☐ Steady Pressure _____ week(s)

   ☐ Fast Carbonation: Shake at _____ p.s.i. for _____ minutes

Beer Storage Temperature: _____

The Final Beer

Chill and test a bottle. If carbonated, you're ready! Otherwise, wait another week and repeat. As you take notes, record how the beer changes as it warms up and lets off more CO_2.

Beer Temperature: _____

Pour Notes (carbonation, head, cloudy, etc.): _____

_____

Aroma Notes (What do you smell from the hops, the malt and the yeast?) _____

_____

_____

Appearance Notes (clarity, color, etc.)

_____

_____

Taste Notes (What tastes do you perceive from the ingredients?)

_____

_____

Mouth Feel/Finish

_____

_____

Overall Notes

_____

_____

_____

Circle all that apply

Bitter   Buttery   Cooked   Sweet   Hoppy   Fruity   Harsh   Malty   Metallic

Spicy   Roasted   Smoky   Watery   Yeasty   Acidic   Sour   Clean   Earthy

Impressions that Change with Temperature/Time: _____

_____

What Worked? _____

_____

What Didn't Work? _____

_____

What Changes Do I Want to Make? _____

_____

_____

Overall Score (0–50) _____

Competition Notes (If you enter the beer in a competition, record the judges' impressions and scores.)

Competition Name: _____

Date: _____ Score: _____ Award: _____

Judge Notes: _____

_____

_____

_____

Competition Name: _____

Date: _____ Score: _____ Award: _____

Judge Notes: _____

_____

_____

_____

Competition Name: _____

Date: _____ Score: _____ Award: _____

Judge Notes: _____

_____

_____

_____

Competition Name: _____

Date: _____ Score: _____ Award: _____

Judge Notes: _____

_____

_____

_____

Recipes for Inspiration

Dead Simple Hefeweizen

Style: German Wheat Beer (Hefeweizen)
Brew Type: Extract
5 gallons
Target OG: 1.048

IBU: 12
Target ABV: 4.7%
60-minute boil

EXTRACT
6.60 pounds — Wheat (Weizen) Liquid Malt Extract (LME)

HOPS
0.5 ounce — Tettnanger — Pellets (4.5 percent AA) for 60 minutes
0.5 ounce — Czech Saaz — Pellets (3.5 percent AA) for 5 minutes

YEAST
White Labs WLP830 Hefeweizen IV, Wyeast 3650 Bavarian Wheat

There's a reason this is "Dead Simple." The longest part of your brew day is boiling the beer. This is an ideal first beer since you can focus on preparing the equipment and process.

Monocle Single Hop Extra Pale Ale

Style: Extra Pale Ale
Brew Type: Extract with Steeped Grains
5 gallons
Target OG: 1.047

IBU: 49
Target ABV: 4.7%
60-minute boil

MALT/GRAIN/SUGAR
0.50 pounds — Belgian Crystal 8L (Caramel Pilsner)

EXTRACT
6.0 pounds — Pale Liquid Malt Extract (LME)

HOPS
1.5 ounces — Cascade — Pellets (5.5 percent AA) for 60 minutes
1.0 ounce — Cascade — Pellets (5.5 percent AA) for 20 minutes
1.0 ounce — Cascade — Pellets (5.5 percent AA) for 0 minutes (at the end of the boil)

OTHER INGREDIENTS
1 tablet — Whirlfloc (or 1 teaspoon Irish Moss) — Added at 20 minutes

YEAST
Wyeast 1056/White Labs WLP001/Fermintis US-05

Extra Pale Ale is an emerging West Coast style. All the hop blast of an IPA is wrapped up in a more imbiber-friendly package. Monocle consists of a bare-bones malt scaffold to hang hops from. If you're going all grain, substitute about 8.5 pounds of American Two-Row malt and mash at 152°F. Fermentation should take less than a week. If the yeast is dropping clear, skip the secondary on the beer and package right away.

Plainweiser Pub Ale

Style: Blonde Ale
Brew Type: Extract
5 gallons
Target OG: 1.037

IBU: 8
Target ABV: 3.7%
60-minute boil

EXTRACT
5.0 pounds   Pale Liquid Malt Extract (LME) (Pilsner preferred)

HOPS
0.25 ounce	Hallertauer Tradition	Pellets (6.0 percent AA) for 60 minutes
0.25 ounce	Czech Saaz	Pellets (3.5 percent AA) for 5 minutes

YEAST
Wyeast 1007 German Ale

Every homebrewer gets asked for a carbon copy of an industrial lager. Even experienced and better-equipped brewers find that a hard target to hit. For now, this recipe gets a beginner in the same zip code!

Tip To suppress the naturally fruity character of ale yeast, ferment this beer at cool temperatures—low to mid-60s—for the first couple of days of fermentation.

Chico West Coast Pale Ale

Style: American Pale Ale
Brew Type: Extract with Steeped Grains
5 gallons
Target OG: 1.059

IBU: 43
Target ABV: 5.9%
60-minute boil

MALT/GRAIN/SUGAR

1.00 pounds	American Two-Row Pale Malt
0.50 pounds	Crystal 60L Malt
0.50 pounds	Honey Malt
0.50 pounds	Aromatic Malt

EXTRACT

6.60 pounds	Pale Liquid Malt Extract (LME)

HOPS

1.0 ounce	Perle	Pellets (8.25 percent AA) for 60 minutes
0.5 ounce	Amarilo	Pellets (8.9 percent AA) for 10 minutes
0.5 ounce	Cascade	Pellets (5.75 percent AA) for 0 minutes (at the end of the boil)

YEAST

American Ale Strain (WLP001, Wyeast 1056, Wyeast 1272, Safale US-05)

MASH SCHEDULE

Steep the malt in 3 quarts of 170°F water for 45 minutes.

American Pale Ale is the beer that built the California micro-brewer. Caramel rich with a citrusy hop nose, the APA was the antidote to decades of yellow, characterless beers.

Tip A standard measurement for liquid malt extract (LME) is 6.6 pounds, because a standard can of LME is 3.3 pounds. If you can't find LME or prefer using dried malt extract, substitute 5.25 pounds of dry for 6.6 pounds liquid.

Kyle's Dry Irish Stout

Style: Irish Stout
Brew Type: Extract with Steeped Grains
5 gallons
Target OG:1.042

IBU: 18
Target ABV: 4.2%
60-minute boil
60-minute boil

MALT/GRAIN/SUGAR

1.00 pounds	Crystal 120L
0.75 pounds	Roasted Barley
0.25 pounds	Black Patent Malt
0.25 pounds	Chocolate Malt

EXTRACT

3.5 pounds	Pale Dry Malt Extract (DME)

HOPS

0.25 ounce	Wye Target	Pellets (10.0 percent AA) for 60 minutes
0.75 ounce	East Kent Goldings	Pellets (4.75 percent AA) for 20 minutes

OTHER INGREDIENTS

2 teaspoons	Calcium carbonate, added to the boil

YEAST

Wyeast 1084 Irish Ale

MASH SCHEDULE

Steep the malt in 3 quarts of 170°F water for 45 minutes.

Stout, the world-famous all day tipple of the old-fashioned Irish punter, is a forgiving style. Between the espresso and chocolate flavors of the roasted malts and the pitch-black color, tasters will be pressed to discern flaws. Fermentation should take less than a week. Skip the secondary on the beer and package right away.

Raucous Red West Coast Ale

Style: American Amber Ale
Brew Type: Extract with Steeped Grains
5.5 gallons
Target OG: 1.050

IBU: 29.3
Target ABV: 4.9%
60-minute boil

MALT/GRAIN/SUGAR

0.50 pounds	CaraMunich 60
0.25 pounds	CaraWheat
0.25 pounds	Aromatic Malt
0.25 pounds	Crystal 120L
0.25 pounds	Honey Malt

EXTRACT

5.50 pounds	Pale Liquid Malt Extract (LME)

HOPS

0.80 ounce	Glacier	Pellets (5.8 percent AA) for 60 minutes
0.60 ounce	Palisade	Pellets (9.4 percent AA) for 20 minutes
5.50 ounces	Amarillo Gold	Pellets (8.9 percent AA) for 0 minutes (at the end of the boil)

OTHER INGREDIENTS

1 tablet	Whirlfloc
1 tablespoon	Yeast Nutrient
1 tablespoon	Gypsum

YEAST

Wyeast 1272 American Ale II

Frankenale

Style: Mega Beer
Brew Type: Partial Mash
5 gallons
Target OG: 1.203

IBU: 382
Target ABV: 23%
90-minute boil

MALT/GRAIN/SUGAR

13.50 pounds	Pale Liquid Malt Extract
4.50 pounds	Domestic Two-Row Pale Malt
0.75 pounds	Cara-Pils Dextrine Malt
0.50 pounds	Flaked Barley
2.00 pounds	Corn Sugar
2.00 pounds	Brown Sugar
2.00 pounds	Honey
1.50 pounds	Turbinado Sugar
1.00 pound	Cane Sugar

HOPS

13.50 ounces	Bullion	Pellets (9.0 percent AA) for 90 minutes
1.50 ounces	Fuggle	Pellets (5.1 percent AA) for 15 minutes
1.50 ounces	Cascade	Pellets (5.4 percent AA) for 2 minutes

OTHER INGREDIENTS

1 tablet	Whirlfloc
1 tablespoon	Yeast Nutrient

YEAST

Wyeast 1056 Chico Ale/WLP001 California Ale/US-05—1 gallon+ Starter or Yeast Cake
Red Star Premier Cuvee (to finish)

MASH SCHEDULE

Saccharification Rest	152°F for 60 minutes

Frankenale

All of the sugars are added slowly over the course of a few weeks. Whenever the fermentation appears to be slowing, boil the sugar in just enough water to dissolve for 15 minutes and add to the carboy. Swirl to mix. Eventually the yeast will cry uncle; hit with rehydrated wine yeast and sit back. It will take around a year to approach drinkable. This recipe is from George Mahoney.

JJ Remix

Style: Rye DIPA
Brew Type: All Grain or Extract with Steeped Grains
5.5 gallons
Target OG: 1.084

IBU: 151.5
Target ABV: 7.9%
120-minute boil

MALT/GRAIN/SUGAR

12.00 pounds	Pale Malt Two-Row
2.00 pounds	Rye Malt
1.00 pound	Munich Malt
0.50 pounds	Aromatic Malt
0.50 pounds	Flaked Rye
0.75 pounds	Rice Hulls
1.50 pounds	Cane Sugar (20 minutes of boil time)

EXTRACT (for 11 pounds of Pale Malt for an extract with steeped grains brew)

7.50 pounds	Pale Liquid Malt Extract (LME)

HOPS

0.50 ounce	Chinook	Pellets (12.0 percent AA) for 90 minutes
1.00 ounce	Columbus	Pellets (16.7 percent AA)for 60 minutes
1.00 ounce	Columbus	Pellets (16.7 percent AA) for 30 minutes
1.00 ounce	Horizon	Pellets (10.0 percent AA) for 15 minutes
1.00 ounce	Columbus	Pellets (16.7 percent AA) for 5 minutes
1.00 ounce	Warrior	Pellets (16.0 percent AA) for 5 minutes
1.00 ounce	Cascade	Pellets (5.2 percent AA) for 0 minutes (at the end of the boil)
2.00 ounces	Amarillo	Whole (10.0 percent AA) for Dry Hopping

OTHER INGREDIENTS

1 tablet	Whirlfloc
1 tablespoon	Yeast Nutrient

YEAST

WLP001 California Ale

MASH SCHEDULE

Saccharification Rest   154°F for 60 minutes

JJ Remix

An example of recipe sharing, the concept originally came from Josh Jensen. He freely provided his recipe that subsequently was "remixed" into a new, rye-infused Double IPA.

Tip Rye has an incredible flavor, but it makes a sticky mash. Rice hulls add lauter insurance. If you're doing a partial mash, definitely use the hulls to supplement all the missing barley hulls.

Boat Weight Water Vapor

Style: California Common
Brew Type: All Grain or Extract with Steeped Grains
5.5 gallons

Target OG: 1.054
IBU: 63.8
Target ABV: 5%
60-minute boil

MALT/GRAIN/SUGAR

9.50 pounds	Pale Malt Two-Row
0.5 pounds	Crystal 60L
0.5 pounds	Vienna Malt

EXTRACT (for 8.5 pounds of Pale Malt for an extract with steeped grains brew)

6.00 pounds	Pale Liquid Malt Extract (LME)

HOPS

1.00 ounce	Northern Brewer	Whole (9.0 percent AA) for 60 minutes
0.50 ounce	Northern Brewer	Whole (9.0 percent AA) for 20 minutes
0.50 ounce	Northern Brewer	Whole (9.0 percent AA) for 5 minutes

OTHER INGREDIENTS

1 tablet	Whirlfloc (for 20 minutes)
1 tablespoon	Yeast Nutrient (for 20 minutes)

YEAST

Wyeast 2112 California Lager (Ferment at 60°F)

MASH SCHEDULE

Saccharification Rest · 153°F for 60 minutes

Boat Weight Water Vapor

California common, traditionally referred to as Steam Beer, is one of the few uniquely American styles of beer. It was created in San Francisco by German immigrants hoping to catch a nugget of the Gold Rush by brewing a warmer lager. If you can't ferment cool, use an American Ale yeast (Wyeast 1056) and make a woody amber ale.

Tip The dying Anchor Brewery was rescued by Fritz Maytag and revitalized over a decade. By that time, Anchor was the last standing maker of San Francisco's unique Steam Beer. Anchor then trademarked the term "Steam Beer."

Gatekeeper Memorial Porter

Style: Robust Porter
Brew Type: All Grain or Steeped Grain Brew
5.5 gallons
Target OG: 1.067

IBU: 31
Target ABV: 6.75%
60-minute boil

MALT/GRAIN/SUGAR

8.00 pounds	Golden Promise/Maris Otter Ale Malt
2.00 pounds	Mild Malt
1.00 pound	Chocolate Malt
6.00 ounces	Crystal 55L
0.25 pounds	Aromatic Malt
0.25 pounds	Black Malt
3.00 ounces	Crystal 150L
2.00 ounces	Biscuit Malt
2.00 ounces	Roasted Barley
2.00 ounces	Special B Malt
2.00 ounces	Special Roast Malt

EXTRACT (for 9 pounds of Maris Otter Malt/Mild Malt for an extract with steeped grains brew)

8.0 pounds	Pale Liquid Malt Extract (LME) (Maris Otter Preferable)

HOPS

1.0 ounce	Fuggle	Pellets (4.5 percent AA) for 60 minutes
1.0 ounce	Fuggle	Pellets (4.5 percent AA) for 30 minutes
1.0 ounce	Fuggle	Pellets (4.5 percent AA) for 5 minutes

OTHER INGREDIENTS

1 tablet	Whirlfloc

YEAST

Wyeast 1318 London III

MASH SCHEDULE

Saccharification Rest	155°F for 60 minutes

Gatekeeper Memorial Porter

Brewed in memory of the brewer's loyal canine assistant, this porter contains a staggering mix of grains to produce a beer of complex character. This recipe is by Curt Stock.

Tip Mild malt is highly kilned pale malt designed to boost body. Think Maris Otter's malty, toasted biscuit and nutty characters turned up higher.

Pater's Uncle Enkel

Style: Belgian "Single"
Brew Type: All Grain
5.5 gallons
Target OG: 1.040

IBU: 14
Target ABV: 3.7%
60-minute boil

MALT/GRAIN/SUGAR

5.50 pounds	Belgian Pale Ale Malt
1.00 pound	Flaked Oats
0.50 pounds	CaraVienne Malt
1.00 pound	Turbinado Sugar

HOPS

0.50 ounce	Styrian Goldings	Pellets (5.4 percent AA) for 60 minutes
0.50 ounce	Styrian Goldings	Pellets (5.4 percent AA) for 15 minutes

OTHER INGREDIENTS

1 tablet	Whirlfloc
1 teaspoon	Yeast Nutrient

YEAST

Wyeast 3864 Canadian Belgian Yeast/Wyeast 1214 Belgian Ale/
WLP550 Belgian Ale

MASH SCHEDULE

Saccharification Rest   153°F for 60 minutes

Enkel is the old term for a trappist single. Patersbier is the beer a Belgian monk drinks with his daily bread. This is a pale version.

Tip To avoid disturbing your set grain bed too much, you need a sparge diffuser. It can be as simple as an upside-down bowl on top of the grain or even better, prodigiously perforated sheets of aluminum foil.